SPIRITUAL LEMONS

Biblical Women, Irreverent Laughter, and Righteous Rage

Rev. Lyn Brakeman

Innisfree
Press, Inc.

A call to the
deep heart's core

Innisfree Press, Inc.
136 Roumfort Road
Philadelphia, PA 19119-1632

Manufactured in the United States of America.

Library of Congress Cataloging-in-Publication Data
Brakeman, Lyn.
    Spiritual lemons : biblical women, irreverent laughter, and righteous rage / by Lyn Brakeman.
        p.   cm.
    Includes bibliographical references (p.).
    ISBN 1-880913-22-4
    1. Women in the Bible—Meditations.   I. Title.
BS575.B64   1997   96-48354
220.9'2'082—dc21   CIP

To the One who freed me to write this book.

Contents

| | Preface | 9 |

Chapter One — **The Spirituality of Laughter** — "Her Last Laugh" — *The story of Sarah in Genesis* — 13

Chapter Two — **The Spirituality of Shame** — "Grace for the Snake" — *The story of the snake in Genesis* — 27

Chapter Three — **The Spirituality of Possessiveness** — "This Is MY Son!" — *The story of Mary, mother of Jesus, in Luke* — 37

Chapter Four — **The Spirituality of Anger** — "Whose Life Is It, Anyway?" — *The story of Jephthah's daughter in Judges* — 47

Chapter Five — **The Spirituality of Powerlessness** — "Oh, Susanna!" — *The story of Susanna in the Apocrypha* — 57

Chapter Six — **The Spirituality of Begging** — "Don't Settle for Any Old Crumbs!" — *The story of the Syrophoenician Woman in Mark* — 71

Chapter Seven — **The Spirituality of Envy** — "He Likes ME Best!" — *The story of Mary and Martha in Luke* — 85

Chapter Eight — **The Spirituality of Death** — "Is Love Enough?" — *The story of the Anointing Woman in Mark* — 97

Suggestions for Personal Prayer and Meditation/ Group Rituals — 109

Acknowledgments

As I contemplated writing acknowledgments, I fell into a trap. It was the all-or-nothing trap. I imagined I either had to acknowledge everyone, from my mother's womb to the Source of all Being, and smear the universe with my gratitude; OR, I could acknowledge no one and eliminate gratefulness altogether. Neither option bears truth. I was denying myself the gift of selectivity.

In that spirit, I acknowledge first my beloved and marriage partner, Richard, the one with the captivating jelly-roll laugh. He has been my chief encourager and is also the one who, on emergency occasions, relinquished the computer seat with grace. He never lapsed into envy, a possible temptation; and, in addition to his cheerleading, became my wisest and most accurate literary critic. I thank him.

I acknowledge with affection and joy my first editor, Lura Jane Geiger. She is the one who believed in me and gave me my first chance at a book. We laughed and groaned through the creative process and shared our faith on the way. Lura has been my midwife. I thank her.

I acknowledge my Spiritual Director, Pierre Wolf. He is a feisty French Jesuit who left his order formally but in spirit, never. Pierre opened to me the Ignatian way of praying with Scripture and dared me to engage with God and with Jesus in profound emotional and bodily ways. It is in this kind of prayer that my midrashim were conceived. Pierre can be pushy. We have disagreed with passion and reconciled with compassion; however, I have never come away from a visit with Pierre without some pearl of new wisdom. He has been my spiritual compassion. I thank him.

I acknowledge my sister, Laurie, a woman of courage and fidelity. She has ridden the waves of this book through smooth and rough seas. Her own creativity is alive and well. She is bonded to me, both in biology and in Christ. I thank her for being my sister.

I acknowledge my second editor, Marcia Broucek. She is a pungent lady, and we have had fun doing the hard editing. Marcia's keen editorial brain awes me. It also helps shape the details and nuances of my prose. Marcia has been enthusiastic and thorough. I thank her.

I acknowledge my mother and my father who gave me human life. They continued to feed me even when, on occasion, my growth hurt them. I thank them for loving me and being my parents.

I acknowledge my friend Lorae Boisvert, who has given her time and trained literary eye to being my "hard reader." More than that, Lorae, along with other friends, has walked with me every step of the way on this bumpy journey. Lorae has been my friend. I thank her.

I acknowledge several Education for Ministry (EFM) students and graduates. They were my "guinea pigs," giving me hours of summer reading time to study my drafts and give me feedback. I know they were too nice at times, but I love them and needed their support just to risk setting sail at all with this endeavor. I thank them all.

I acknowledge my several psychotherapists along the way. All have gently demanded that I be and love myself. It is with their help that I came to know the God in whom I live and move and have my being. I thank them.

I acknowledge my children and stepchildren (and a couple of spouses), all beautiful people. They have touched in and out of this process with humor, alacrity, and always admiration, tinged at times with incredulity. My favorite representative comment is, "Mom, you mean this will actually be in a bookstore?!" These are my next generation. I love them and thank them.

Finally, I acknowledge Madeleine L'Engle, and David Whyte, and too many other women and men writers to mention, whose work I have read with avarice and whose voices have persuaded me to use my own voice. They have been my inspirations. I thank them.

Preface

Why did you pick up a book about spiritual lemons? To see how tangy it was? Or just to satisfy your curiosity? Maybe you felt some righteous rage of your own. Or it could be that it tickled your spiritual funny-bone and you just had to indulge your own irreverent laughter. Whatever the reason, I hope you will read it to find out about yourself and your spirituality, from the most surface to the most deep.

I have a friend who is a voicer of organ pipes. As he describes the intricate and delicate process of shaping a pipe to give proper voice to a range of sound, I am in awe. How much behind-the-scenes gift, patience, skill, and love it takes to make beautiful sounds precise! Lots of women are good voicers. And God is a voicer of women as well as men. It's time those unsung voices among us sang out!

I have chosen to write about women, both ancient and modern, because I hope that women today will connect their own passions with those of the unsung biblical women. As women, we need to know the importance of our bodies and our voices in the ongoing work of God.

I have also chosen to write about the "underbelly" of spirituality, about the scandals of Scripture: Sarah dares to laugh in God's face, Jephthah's daughter organizes a resistance movement, Mary and Martha fight, the Syrophoenician woman confronts Jesus, and Susanna challenges the Bible itself!

Imagine opening the spiritual "gift box" looking for love, joy, and peace, and, instead, finding anger, envy, shame, possessiveness, powerlessness, begging, laughter—even the dreaded angel of death! These gifts are spirituality turned upside-down.

These are the fruits of the Spirit—love, joy, peace, patience, kindness, goodness, faithfulness, gentleness, self-control (Galatians 5:22)—turned rotten! These are the non-gifts we pray to be rid of. Pandora's pandemonium! Maybe we should slam the box shut.

Instead, I want to encourage women—and men—to open the gift box all the way, to accept all parts of themselves as gift, and to direct all their passions honestly toward God in prayer and in action for justice. We need to love our down side. We need to know that God loves and uses all our parts, especially those we ourselves would keep secret and those that society would condemn—the "lemons."

The zest of a lemon is at times called for in cooking to assure the full flavor. That's as true for the spiritual life as it is for gourmet dishes. This book is *not* about making lemonade when life deals out lemons. It is *not* about sweetening up the sour. It is about *full-flavored spirituality*.

It seems to me that women, or any group that is oppressed systemically and systematically, will naturally live with chronic negative feelings such as anger, shame, envy, despair, and will too often have to settle for less than their due. One way a ruling class ideology makes sure such groups stay oppressed and disempowered is to define such feelings as "unacceptable" and consign them to the spiritual vice list. The threat of social and moral exile can stop even the most sanguine from fighting back. This book is about naming and claiming some of those feelings that have been damned. This book is about finding the courage to bear witness to the spiritual fruit that unpopular and difficult feelings can bear: holy if tangy!

God dignifies what humanity rejects. The scandal is this: Transformation is not a condition for divine acceptance; nor is it a necessary outcome for spiritual wholeness. Lemons stay lemons. Know and loved on their own terms, lemons can be life-savers! Difficult feelings can become toxins trapped in the human soul, but, when touched by the Spirit of love and acceptance, they can be instruments of love, justice, and peace. They can make us and our communities whole.

I have chosen the midrash form for this endeavor because of its flexibility, playfulness, and humor. It's a very fleshy genre! The Hebrew root of midrash is *darash*, which means to seek, search, or demand. Most midrash is Jewish; there isn't much Christian midrash. I think we need to take risks to liberate the Scriptures from the stuffy closets of untouchable holiness, excessive spiritualization, and ruling-class orthodoxy.

The goal of midrash is immersion into the divine Word, getting it into our bones. As we draw more and more stories out of the story, we bond our stories to the original story. To do midrash is to demand meaning from the biblical text, to ask it to take flesh. That's why midrash always begins with a question asked of the text. It's not intellectual exegesis; it's a spiritual experience. You practically have to drown in the story, drinking it in until it slakes your spiritual hunger and thirst and forces you to grow. Midrash puts flesh on the bones of the text and makes it alive.

Midrash is also a way to approach the Bible without academic intimidation. Anyone can do it. Spiritually, the midrashic process recalls the Wisdom/Sophia figure[1] in Proverbs who plays with God, delighting in the creative process. She is characterized as the feminine spirit present with God, creating and enlivening human souls and inviting us to her banquet. She is the one who, in Jewish Wisdom literature, enters into relationship with us and guides us into truth. She is a depth charge to

1   For more on the Sophia/Wisdom tradition, see Elizabeth Johnson's *She Who Is*, Crossroad, New York, 1994.

the human spirit, blessing and calling forth absolutely everything she finds. There is nowhere she will not go, and she is not fussy about whose flesh she occupies for the sake of the reign of God!

Doing midrash is like tossing the Word into the air like so many rubber balls to see what new formation will emerge, what new enchantment will be revealed. I have found that to play with God and to plunge the depths with Wisdom/Sophia is like taking a breath of spiritual fresh air. In this polluted age, it is nice to be able to inhale deeply and replace the dense smoke of our unlit but smoldering passions with the life of God. I hope you too will feel refreshed and enlivened and taste the "lemons" in your own life without puckering up.

To expand your exploration and experience of these biblical women, consider the Suggestions for Personal Prayer and Meditation given at the end of the book. I would also encourage you to gather in small groups to study and share the contents of this book. If you have this opportunity, the Suggested Group Ritual for each chapter will focus and enrich your experience together.

The Spirituality of Laughter

Laughter is to life as paprika is to ghoulash: Laughter makes life piquant. It is the spice that causes the taste buds to burst open and fill the mouth with flavor. It makes us pucker up, then burst open to fill the air with joy.

There are many kinds of laughter, from sadistic sniggers to belly laughs. They don't all mean the same thing. Some signal danger and some inflict wounds. But you can tell a safe laugh by how it makes you feel. If you feel like laughing yourself, it's probably safe. If you feel like pretending to laugh to feel safe, it's probably not.

Ultimately, laughter is spiritual because it creates a space for God to enter more fully, resurrecting life. God's laughter is like thunder. It burbles and rumbles and builds to a mighty crescendo. Then it blasts open the heavens, boundless energy without reserve. It clears the air completely. It's a resurrection! . . . the last laugh.

O

Her Last Laugh

Then one [of the three men who appeared to Abraham representing the Lord God, Yahweh] *said, "I will surely return to you in due season, and your wife Sarah shall have a son."*

And Sarah was listening at the tent entrance . . . it had ceased to be with Sarah after the manner of women. So Sarah laughed to herself . . .

The Lord said, . . . "Why did Sarah laugh?" . . .

But Sarah denied, saying, . . . "I did not laugh" . . .

God [sic] *said, "Oh yes, you did laugh."* (Genesis 18:10-15)

Abraham was a hundred years old when his son Isaac was born. Now Sarah said, "God has brought laughter for me; everyone who hears will laugh with me." (Genesis 21:5-6)

O

What makes Sarah laugh?

O

If there was one thing Sarah could always muster, it was a good hearty laugh. She was famous for it. People liked her to provide the laughter. When she was a little girl, her Papa called her "my child of mirth." "It is a gift from Yahweh," he would tell her, "this ability you have to get a God's eye view of reality."

The spirit of Sarah's laughter rivaled the depth, width,

and breadth of the cosmos. It allowed her to see the absurd peculiarities of human foible and the puny poignancy of human effort. Sarah laughed with Yahweh.

It wasn't that Sarah lacked compassion. In fact, her laughter often mingled with tears. Together, the tears and the laughter formed a precarious emotional bridge between individual pathos and the cosmic comic drama of Being itself. To Sarah, the pitiful efforts of a single ant to extricate the body of a loved one from being annihilated by a big human foot was as tragic as it was comic, as ultimately essential as it was ultimately peripheral.

That's how Sarah saw her beloved Abraham, as an ant: compulsively faithful, plodding, carving out a Tradition among his people. He posed as a patriarch, a chieftain of a band of scruffy nomads. His relentless faith in the covenant promises of Yahweh was both touching and ridiculous. Sarah laughed.

Sarah's faith was different, less intense, even bordering on lax. Her God was a mystery of absurd paradox, a God with whom one *must* laugh. Some people mistook her laughter for a faithless laughter. They were wrong. Sarah only laughed *with* Yahweh, not *at* Yahweh. Others found her laughter impertinent. Abraham found her fluidity a trial. She would chuckle, realizing her importunate laughter both charmed and vexed him.

When the three messengers of Yahweh came to visit, they brought an annunciation of huge moment. Abraham said so. But Sarah laughed. Abraham tried to hush her, as he scurried around antishly, preparing a grandiose meal and soliciting her help. This only made her laugh more. Imagine fussing so about hospitality protocol in the presence of Divine Beings! Sarah did attempt that day, for the sake of her love for Abraham, to stifle her glee; however, she let out an especially loud full-bellied, carillon of broad-sided laughter when the messengers told her she would become pregnant. That was too much. Abraham laughed at that, too, although he tried to keep it all dignified, attending to the messengers with proper respect.

"Abraham, my love," Sarah squeezed out her words between bursts of giggle. "Imagine! Listen to what Yahweh is planning now! Sex at our age—and with procreation attached, yet. I don't know which is funnier. Of course, I think Yahweh can do this. Yahweh can do anything . . . and does! That's why I laugh. My laughter signals the presence of God. Don't you see? Ha! Yahweh IS my laugh!"

"But seriously, dear," Sarah continued in whispers, "You don't think Yahweh would do this to me, do you?"

The thought of such a disaster at her age caused Sarah's faith to slip into fear for a brief moment. It was the only time Sarah did not laugh *with* Yahweh. In fact, she tried to deny that she had even laughed at all.

But the Wise Old One said right back, "Ah, but you *did* laugh."

And Yahweh was right. Sarah had laughed.

She continued to whisper with Abraham. "Sex, okay, but pregnancy and a child to rear? At my age? No! What misery that would be. What an impossibility. Why, being pregnant could be the one thing that would take away my joy and my laughter."

And it did.

God's ridiculous promise was no laughing matter. Sarah was too old to be going through pregnancy. People had always told her that sometimes the ways of Yahweh involved suffering, but this felt like it would crush her. She was unable to find the laughter in her limitations. She was miserable in soul and body.

"What possible good can this bring, oh Yahweh?" she prayed. "I know you do absurdities, but this is too much. The pain is all over my body. My body cannot support such a thing. There's not an inch of me at peace. I ache. I cannot walk. My belly and all parts of me are swollen. And I cannot laugh. I have lost my gift. Oh, Yahweh of Hosts, I used to laugh in faith. I used to laugh with you when you showed us our littleness. Mine was the laughter of belief, not disbelief. You made laughter for me. You gave it to me as a spiritual gift. But where is my laughing now? Oh, Yahweh, at least restore my laughter, especially if I am to survive this pregnancy. Losing my laughter is what pains me most."

But Sarah did not laugh. Her God had turned sour on her, she thought, and she was afraid. Abraham was no comfort, so caught up was he in the miracle, the promised child. He didn't even think of how hard it was for her to carry this promise in her belly and bear its weight in her groin!

"Promises, promises," Sarah grumbled to Yahweh. "I see no promise for me. I won't even live to see my child grown. Abraham gets all the credit, and he is not the one who has to live in this wretched state. I'm too old for this! And surely you know that late babies rarely survive and are often malformed and mental idiots. Haven't you heard? Where is your cosmic common sense? What a laugh! Come on and laugh with me, old Yahweh."

She managed a laugh, but it had no lilt, no music.

Against all odds, Sarah gave birth to a healthy and beautiful son. Her milk flowed in abundance from her aged and pendulous breasts. She named her son "Isaac," which meant "he who laughs." She hoped the naming would deliver her from her depression and restore her to laughter through her son.

Abraham was exuberant with blessing. Sarah was grateful. Yahweh had blessed her. She realized again how aware Yahweh was of the sheer antishness of human life. Yet in spite of all these blessings, Sarah still could not laugh. Her depression enshrouded her body. She did derive some pleasure from her child's life and laughter, but her own laughter had died and, with it, her soul and her faith.

Things got worse and worse. Sarah's depression continued into the early months of Isaac's infancy. Sarah became so dispossessed of her laughing faith that she began to abuse her innocent maidservant, Hagar. Although Sarah felt guilty for it, she couldn't seem to help herself. She was eaten alive inside, possessed by rancor. She hated Hagar and her healthy little son, Ishmael. What made it even worse was that Hagar was actually Sarah's favorite and brightest servant, almost a friend. That's why Sarah, when it hadn't seemed possible she would ever conceive, had once chosen Hagar to lie with Abraham. But, in the end, Sarah forced Abraham against his will to banish both Hagar and Ishmael. Sarah was a woman gone mad.

Sarah missed the laughter but was too lifeless even to pray for its return. She could only sit in her tent mumbling a few inarticulate groanings. At one point she actually moaned aloud with cavernous sighs, too low for ears, too sad for hearts.

And the Lord God Yahweh heard her cry.

Sarah emerged out of her gloom at the sound of Abraham's prayer. He was at a distance, but she heard him as clearly as if he were at her side. Strange, since her old ears weren't that acute anymore. Abraham was disputing with God, a skill he had developed and refined over the years as he had struggled to remain faithful and keep his people adherent to the covenant relationship with Yahweh, a relationship from which they readily strayed.

Sarah sat straight up and listened. She felt energy in her bones. She hadn't felt it for years. It chilled and thrilled her. She heard Abraham pleading with Yahweh not to put him to the test, to spare his son's life, to find another way, a more merciful way, as Yahweh had on so many other occasions. Abraham was a fine debater, and his arguments were impeccable, but it seemed to Sarah that he was losing. Isaac's life was in danger. All of a sudden, she laughed.

"Ah, Yahweh, my God, such a time for laughter to

return!" Sarah clapped her hand to her mouth as she prayed. "You are funnier than I ever thought. What a time for deliverance!"

Sarah knew that Yahweh was again in her laughter. She didn't yet understand how, but she knew this laughter meant God at work.

"What are you up to now, Yahweh? This can't be a test. The you I know doesn't do that, even though Abraham thinks you do, despite what I tell him about you. He never listens." Sarah stood up, eager with anticipation.

"Oh, I forgot to thank you for my laughter," she said laughing. "Thank you. Now listen while I pray, for the gift of prayer is restored to my lips through laughter. The situation is dire, as you can see. Abraham is faithful to a fault—like an ant. He believes it is your desire that he make an offering of Isaac. *Is this your desire?*"

Yahweh laughed.

"That's what I thought," Sarah grinned. "But there's still the problem of Abraham and your respect for his freedom. But, of course, you are free to make me your servant in this matter, too! And then there's the problem of Abraham and his theology. Abraham thinks this is your desire, he calls it your WILL. I won't be able to dissuade him. His own will is very strong and even more set than yours, Holy One. I, as you know, think differently from my beloved marriage partner of the years. I believe your will is your deepest desiring for me, the same as I desire for myself when I am in touch with my best instincts. Abraham thinks a bit more juridically, as if your will were a law outside him. This thinking serves him well sometimes but not all of the time. You have taught me another way. You have shown me that your will is like a gentle flow of Spirit in my life, like a stream, always moving along over rocks and falls and resting in deep clear pools, but never staying its course toward the vast ocean of your Love.

And this stream, of course, laughs as it goes, laughing all the way to you."

As Sarah talked and laughed with Yahweh, reveling in the new life she felt, she also was increasingly alert to the danger her son was in. He could be sacrificed for naught. She could lose him. This she knew was not Yahweh's desire. But Abraham was *that* faithful!

"Funny man," she smiled as she thought of Abraham. "But let's get serious here, Yahweh—serious. We need a plan, a plan good enough to call Abraham's discernment up short, to pull him back into your living waters. Abraham loves his son, and so he will listen readily to any plan that might save Isaac, but it has to be something that will speak to his faith in you. You have to speak big and loud here, not just a little internal nudge. Usually, it doesn't take much with Abraham. He's a God-says-and-we-go man! But he sees this as a test of his faith. Abraham would die for you. He has to hear that his faith is affirmed—just a little off course, that's all. So can we do it? Can we save our son, yours by promise and mine by flesh? Oh, incidentally, I hope you forgive me my loss of faith and all. You know it's miserable to be pregnant and bear a child at my age! I also forgive you for the pain your laughable little scheme caused me and my body." Sarah laughed.

So Sarah and Yahweh made a plan. Sarah's part seemed to her a bit harder than Yahweh's part, especially at her age! All Yahweh had to do was assign an angel to get Abraham's attention, deter the execution, and thank him for his good faith. She knew Yahweh would do this. Sarah was that faithful.

For her part, she had to arrange to get a ram up to one of the mountains of Moriah and make sure it was well lodged by its horns in the thickets. It had to be exactly positioned so Abraham would see it; and further, it had to be plump and perfect, according to the code of ethics for offerings. Then she had to prod it in a timely fashion to encourage it to make enough noise to attract Abraham's attention. All this had to be done without being seen, following Abraham at a distance so the ram would end up on the correct mountain. It was a laughable series of tasks.

"Such a mission . . . and at my age!" Sarah couldn't help laughing again.

Then she hurried to her tasks. She got some good and faithful servants to help her. They were puzzled but cooperative. They had learned that Sarah's voice carried as much authority as Abraham's. And they were also pleased to see their mistress laughing and alive again.

Sarah silently wished for Hagar, who had always been her best and most canny companion, and the only one she could laugh with. She felt a pang of sorrow and uttered a prayer for forgiveness for what she had done to her friend. She trusted Yahweh would take care of Hagar and her son.

Up the mountain they went, ram in tow, Sarah laughing and praying all the way but not making too much noise, for fear Abraham would notice. But Abraham and Isaac heard nothing. Abraham was too self-absorbed in his grief, and Isaac was delighting in the father/son outing.

Sarah hid to watch, eager to rejoice in the outcome. She knew she had done her part well. She knew Yahweh would do well, too. She began to get a little nervous, though, because Yahweh waited until the last minute to intervene.

Sarah gasped, "My God, the knife is poised already. Let's go!"

Then she heard Yahweh's laughter, and she knew the deed was accomplished as planned.

Sarah laughed and cried all the way home.

O

NOTE: To read all of Sarah's story in the Bible, see Genesis 16–Genesis 23:2.

Commentary

It makes me laugh to notice how little laughter is recorded in the Jewish and Christian Scriptures. Is our God really so mirthless? Surely people must have laughed, if for no other reason than to maintain their sanity in the midst of the difficult challenges and impossible calls they discerned to be from their God. Did biblical editors and scribes fear that including people's jocularity might diminish the seriousness of divine/human matters? Did they edit the laughter out?

I did a little research about this because it seemed to me that Sarah was the only one directly recorded as laughing. For good reason, she laughed at the idea that she and her husband would be having sexual pleasure *and* procreating a child at ages when such things went well beyond their expected natural capacities. I would have laughed, too. The whole idea is portrayed as another one of Yahweh's preposterous schemes.

My research indicated that there is not much recorded laughter in the Bible. But I did find in the story of Daniel that he is recorded as laughing aloud at the king's worship of worthless idols. His laughter endangered his life. Like Sarah's laugh, his was the laughter of faith in God, even in impossible situations. And then there is Mary. I wonder if she laughed, along with her pondering and questioning, at the idea that her child was to be conceived by the Holy Spirit: sexual intercourse with God? Awesome, and certainly worth a belly laugh!

But, for the most part, when the word "laughter" is used in Scripture, it generally refers to the laughter of disbelief and derision. In Job, the innocent laughed at unbelievers; believers in God laughed off famine and disaster; and Leviathan laughed mockingly at the impotence of hurled javelins that could not stem his power. This kind of laughter is the fearless laughter of the faithful who trust in God and, with Yahweh, "laugh to scorn" unrighteous opposing forces (Wisdom 4:18). In the Psalms, God laughed in derision and at the wicked, and the enemies of the faithful laughed in hostility (37:13). Laughter is also cited as the response of a people wondrously saved (Psalm 126:2), and laughter was the reward of repentance for Job (8:21) The preacher of Ecclesiastes warned that laughter in the face of grim reality was mad (2:2; 7:3-6). And in the Wisdom literature, laughter is associated with merriment at good fortune and feasting. It is the opposite of sorrow and lamenting.

Christian testament citations of laughter are few. The most direct laughing occurred when Jesus told the crowds that Jairus' daughter was not dead but sleeping. They laughed at him (Luke 8:53). It is hard to tell if this is the laughter of scorn or of glee at the idea of a divine intervention. I suspect the former.

And then there was the reaction of Jesus' followers to the news of the resurrection (a laughable event at one level): their "disbelief for joy" (Luke 24:41, RSV). For Christians who don't laugh much in church or nearly enough in our faith, I think laughter can help us cope with this painful crucifixion event at the center of our faith. Laughter does not take away from the seriousness of the pain but enables us to see that there is more than the pain. Can't you imagine Jesus' followers laughing when they finally discerned there had been a resurrection? This kind of joy contains the paradoxical laughter of faith: Faith that credits God with miraculous achievement and laughs, as boldly as Sarah did, at the joy of God's promise to bring life out of death. At the same time, this faith remains rooted firmly in sensory human experience and laughs, as freely as Sarah did, to affirm our humanity.

When we, like Sarah, can identify laughter as a gift from

God (Genesis 21:5-6), we can know that God penetrates into and through our experience with wondrous accuracy and grace. We can know that, no matter how strange, painful or unfathomable our circumstances may be, God is present with us in the living out of it all in faith.

I like to think of properly, and even improperly, placed laughter as a spiritual gift, even though Paul didn't put it on his "gift list" (Galatians 5:22-23). I am sure that Jesus must have laughed, not to mock unbelievers but to praise God. And certainly, even now, we are learning more and more about the benefits of laughter. Norman Cousins, in his *Anatomy of an Illness*, describes the healing effect of laughter on the human soul and body. It is not that Cousins laughs at illness or laughs it away in denial; it is simply that he laughs while he is also ill.

In my own life, the gift of laughing has always been salvific when it is not discounting of my reality. It saves me when it provides a larger perspective on the scene. My marriage partner has a wildly robust laugh. Sometimes it is just plain ribald and annoys me, especially if I am caught up in my own seriousness. But his is the kind of laughter that transports everyone around him into a circle of merriment and joy. It is contagious and a blessing. It is a spiritual gift. He has the ability to laugh at himself in moments of awkwardness and in the middle of his own pathos. His laugh, at times, has such a ring of truth and authenticity that it can bring us both to freedom in the middle of a battle. One of us will say something so irrational that he peals off into fits of laughing at the sheer funniness of it. When he laughs like that, he brings the quality of mercy not scorn, and I cannot help but follow him. Laughter breaks the tension and moves us back into right relationship. Then the two of us can begin to resolve our dispute, most always with equity and love.

Seeing the comic in life without ridicule, we mortals can have a sense of the Holy, a kind of awe and wonder at the significance of our littleness and the littleness of our significance. Laughter also makes tragedy bearable. Perhaps laughter is even a gift God gives us not to deny sin and evil, nor to laugh it off, but to prevent its dominance. I imagine this was the spirit of Sarah's laughter in the midst of her pretty tough life. I imagine laughter empowered her in faith and possibly in the saving of her son. I especially imagine that laughter was one of the ways she connected with her beloved Yahweh.

The Spirituality of Shame

As a child, I blushed. It was an outer sign of an invisible disgrace, a deep felt sense of unworthiness. It happened when the teacher called on me. I knew the answer, but there went my cheeks anyway! Let me disappear, God, I would pray.

In Spanish to be called *"sinvergüenza,"* which literally means "without shame," is an insult. To be without shame is shameful. Shame shames itself: the soul against itself.

Shame is a treasure, a sacrament. It reminds us that we are earthen vessels, that our bodies can shrivel at the rise of a parental eyebrow, that our souls can be recreated by a fleshy God.

I love winter trees. Some people prefer trees in leafy dress, but I am drawn to naked winter trees. Shame is like the nakedness of those trees. In their nakedness, I can see their true shape.

O

Grace for the Snake

*The Lord God said to the serpent, "Because you
have done this, cursed are you among all animals
and among all wild creatures; upon your belly you
shall go, and dust you shall eat all the days of your
life. I will put enmity between you and the woman,
and between your offspring and hers . . .*
(Genesis 3:14-15a)

O

Why do women hate snakes?
Why, for that matter, does God?

O

She was old, ready to die . . . and not ready to die. She'd lived
with her question all the length of her days. Now she supposed
she would have to die with it—the question, that is. The question about snake grace. Why, from the beginning, was there no
break for the snake?

As often as her lifelong question recurred, so did her
anger. She never could understand how there seemed to be some
grace for everyone but the snake. Why did the snake have to live
in eternal shame like this? Her anger had lived secretly within
her like a clenched fist all her days, and every so often it expelled
a bit of its venom like a shot out of a time-released capsule: bitter
pill, bitter pill.

"It isn't fair," she grumbled to herself, coiling and recoil-
ing. "Why would God, if there even *is* a God, lay it heavier on

us snakes? We, after all, are part of creation, and we, too, were called good. Or so it says in their Good Book. Why is our sin any worse than any others'? Bad enough the notoriety, but to be a *cosmic* scapegoat is awful! Simply awful!"

She curled up tight on her rock, trying to short circuit the electric shock of hot shame that surged throughout her entire length. She'd hoped that the pain might abate with age.

"For scapegoats, shame is an everlasting hot flash!" she grunted.

In her aging there wasn't the dignity there ought to be. It was small consolation to be considered a *grande dame* by some of her kind.

"Imagine the arrogance of blaming a snake for the whole messy affair anyway! Fools!" she hissed. "It wasn't our fault. The humans surely hold some responsibility for their actions. But God at least gave them clothes when they were judged and thrown out of the garden. A token gesture to be sure, but still a sign of divine grace, minimalist love. All we snakes got was a curse. Curses bear bad fruit: heaps of undeserved scorn and people's phobic reactions. Of course, there is *some* delight in the power to scare people, but, really, the consequences of our action have, over time, had a magnitude clearly disproportionate to our crime. All we did was tell a half-truth, make the humans think before they disobeyed or obeyed. Subtlety like this has merit. Wiliness is a kind of canny wisdom, a gift when used well by those of the so-called *weaker* sex . . . and asps. That's one of our other names, you know."

She rolled over in disgust, taking little pleasure in her insights and trying to shed her discomfort as she lay on the rock by the pond. The sun felt good. It was warm, bright. She felt cradled. She resumed her rememberings. They soothed her.

"Once we serpents (another one of our names) had our Golden Age. Once we were symbols of fertility and life—eternal life, no less. Ha! They thought because we shed our skins and came up new every time that we had secret powers of generativity. We used to chuckle. We knew it was just us, how we were made, how God made us. That's all—no more, no less. We used to be pals with the first human woman—almost goddess status, we were. Now women step on our necks!"

Aided by the sun's brightness, the old snake lifted her neck from her coil to preen, hoping to bedazzle her Creator. Laughing, she shot a slanty glance skyward, trying to catch the divine eye. "Ah, me. I wonder if the Old Creator cares at all. How could God be such a turncoat?"

The thought of such betrayal and shaming fell heavily on her sunny-side-upness. She sagged back down into her coil. What made it worse was that she was bothered by all this far more than the others in her family. They all laughed at her question.

"Grace? For a snake?" they would wiggle in giggles.

They told her she was far too serious and shrugged her off. This they did openly when she was young. Now they did it on the sly, apparently deferential to her status while secretly sloughing off her obsession like so much snakeskin. It hurt. Not to be credible added to her shame.

"Maybe something is wrong with me," she thought. "No average asp. Alas, I shall die in my poisonous juices." The thought depressed her.

She wondered as her eyes drooped half-shut, "Why? Why do I think of God so much? The others don't. They have let God go, paid no heed to the matter. After all, you can't see God . . . only a misty presence, a regular ghost!"

God seemed like an absurd idea to her kin, especially since God had no substance. How could you believe in something that could not be seen or heard or touched?

"Pooh!" she sighed. "They're right . . . God is nothing but myth!"

And yet she wondered and wondered. Perhaps serpents had taken things *too* literally over the ages. She'd been taught not to pray. It was against snake rules. You didn't pray to a nobody. And there was *no* body. They were right. Their facts were indisputable.

"But there has to be more to it," she thought. "There is truth here . . . perhaps. But what is *truth*?"

They had never taught her the word, but she knew it anyway. She shifted restlessly on the rock, unable to get comfortable. The rock was like this cloudpuff of a God. It just wouldn't conform to her shape, but its solidity was an absolute necessity for sun-bathing and soul-searching.

"I mean what was so bad about our part in the Eden affair? Why is snake sin any more scandalous than the human sin of eating the damned fruit? Surely that was a more direct affront to the Almighty! All one of our kind did was expose the subtleties of the matter. A snake—probably a female, else why all the scandal—told them the facts of the case. You can't argue with facts! She, ancient bearer of the curse, one of my own ancestors, told Adam and Eve they would not die, as God had said they would, if they ate of the fruit. And they didn't die. That's the fact. We snakes were literally right. Clever and wily . . . AND right!"

All this she thought. All this she did not believe.

"Well, we were half-right, at least," she soothed her aching old conscience. "In truth, they did die after they ate. They lost their secure connection with the God of their very life. They knew then how to do wrong and feel bad—the death of innocence. We snakes were half-wrong, too. Oh, who cares!" her pique gave way to gastric distress. "I'm old now and olding. Who cares now?"

"I care," she thought. "I care."

Suddenly, without conscious consent, coming from deep

within her, unwilled, unsought, scarcely permitted, inarticulate,
and out of her charge, came her prayer:

> Oh God, my God. I have known the truth of your
> being from the beginning, and I have lied to
> myself and to you. I am old. I am sad. I am angry.
> I know you are there, dimly, in shadow forms.
> Answer my question, if you will. Where is re-
> demption for the snake? Where is your love for
> me, God? Do you love me a little, too? Do you
> care for us asps? Why were we included in the
> goodness of Creation if not to be graced, if not to
> be loved?

If not to be loved. If not to be loved . . .

The effort exhausted her, and she lay motionless on her
rock. Through the slit of one eye she watched the sun fade.

And the Lord God spoke to her in the cool of the evening.

"Sister snake," the Lord God said. "You are my created
one. I have heard your cry. There *is* snake grace of a very
particular kind. Do not shame your shame. There has always
been grace for you—in the disgrace of your belly itself. Have you
not known this? Have you not seen? Remember, my beloved, no
one can trip a snake. You can't trip a snake!"

A divine belly laugh shook the heavens with merriment
and faded away.

The old one was startled awake. Anger flashed through
her length and passed right on out. And then she smiled. She
found herself laughing in an oldish way, then giggling like a
young girl ablossoming. She felt stripped naked with delight.

"Oh, my. At last a word from God," she chuckled. "And
what a Word! I know it is God. Who else but the great Creator
could know the exact bite of snake humor? 'You can't trip a
snake,' indeed! Who but the One who made us knows us? Who

but the One who made me *me?*"

Comforted, she fell asleep on her sun-warmed, soul-soaked rock.

O

NOTE: To read the snake's story in the Bible, see Genesis 2:4b–Genesis 3.

Commentary

It all began at a writers' workshop. We were asked to pick a person in the Bible who seemed angry and write about it. The snake coiled into my thoughts, and angry feelings came up. I recalled times I had felt like a scapegoat: sad, lonely, guilty, and inadequate, as if everything were my fault. I remembered times when I had spoken out in my family about some truth that had seemed obvious to me, and I had ended up being ostracized. No one else was willing or able to see what I saw.

Even now I can feel the burning of my shame.

Shame reminds me of the burning bush Moses saw: It burned hot and was never consumed. Shame never completely ends. I used to think if it weren't for my big mouth, things would be fine! And with that thought, I denied my own truth and kept the shame burning on. I blushed on for years. Just as the burning bush called Moses' attention to God's call, my blush calls me to God, calls me to wake up to my true self and trust God's love. Maybe this is what Moses found, too: his worth through the image of the burning bush. Perhaps the bush served as an outer symbol of his inner shame: his feelings of inadequacy about being a murderer called by God to lead his people. Perhaps Moses' shame was put right into the sanctifying fire of divine love. Perhaps the burning bush of shame even made it possible for Moses—and for me—to know God.

There is an ancient prayer, the *Anima Christi*, that reads, "Passion of Christ, strengthen me. O good Jesu, hear me; Within thy wounds hide me . . ." It reminds me that God has carved out a place for our shame in the life of Jesus. Shame, the curse that comes to the innocent not from God but from the scorn of the world, is hidden and healed in the consoling safety of Jesus' own shameful wounds.

How did I get away from snakes? There's a connection here. It has to do with shame and healing and love.

The obvious truth that the Eden asp discerns is the classist *hubris* of the human creatures in the garden. They forego the boundaries of their creaturely status and reach for equality with God. But no one appreciates the snake's perspicacity. She is roundly cursed and stigmatized for all time for her successful attempt to prove she is right.

Did God really hate snakes? Is this how God really felt, I wonder? Does God curse and excommunicate forever? It doesn't sound like the God I know. Is there some other, human, agenda creeping into the Genesis story? What would an encounter between the Creator of the universe and the creator of the Fall be like? These questions add to my disgruntlement at the plight of the asp.

Not too long ago, the serpentine plot surfaced for me again in an Education for Ministry group I was mentoring. We were reflecting theologically on the Genesis story and searching for the redemption in it.

Someone snorted, "Well, there certainly can't be any grace for the snake!"

And someone else quipped, "Ah, but remember, you can't trip a snake."

This wonderful phrase became the group's theological motto and helped us to stay compassionate with ourselves and others who might be unjustly stigmatized and scapegoated. It helped us remember to seek for grace in things we are told even God can't abide. It helped us with our shame. It helped us also to remember to seek for balance in the emotional seesaw of shame and blame. (And, it also gave me my punch line for this midrash!)

After I wrote the midrash, I used it in a sermon one Sunday. It was then that I realized the deeper pathos of the serpent condition. Afterward, a woman came to me with many tears, hardly able to talk. She identified profoundly with the snake and felt the grace of God touching her own hidden, snakelike shame.

This prompted some further research into the snake. I wondered if the snake had always been in such disfavor. I discovered, to my joy, that she had not. I discovered that in ancient times she had a close association with Woman, the very one with whom enmity was declared in the Genesis story. The serpent is one of the oldest symbols of female power. Women and snakes together were considered holy in preclassic Aegean civilization. It is true that the Hebrew Scriptures associate the serpent with evil and with being the cause of our expulsion from paradise. However, before the patriarchal reworking in Genesis, the serpent was associated with the Great Goddess whose image had *nothing* to do with evil. The connection of the snake with Woman has to do with creativity itself. Snakes were believed to be immortal because they shed their skins and renewed their life regularly. The birthing power of women was perceived similarly as self-generating fertility and primordial life force. Such powers are to be revered or feared, maybe even banished. I choose reverence!

A lot has happened to women and snakes since those ancient times. We have not been consumed in our burning bushes of shame!

I dedicate this midrash to women everywhere who have used their shame for self-knowing and have found their way out from under trumped up "charges." I envision these redeemed women, along with snakes, dancing together in the heart of God . . . untrippable!

The Spirituality of Possessiveness

I always thought that possessiveness was something bad. The word definitely does not have a good reputation! I think of the words "MINE" and "MY" and recall little hands being slapped and told to "SHARE." But, oh, I remember too what powerful satisfaction those words had in my soul. This is MINE! This is MY toy, MY dress, MY word, MY experience. These things were not negotiable. Possessiveness felt solid as a rock.

I also used to think possessiveness in relationships was bad—until I met God. God is jealous, very possessive indeed. And so much in love! God calls us and names us and makes us God's own. God says all the time, over and over: "You are MINE; you are MY people." It has a wonderful ring. It makes me feel safe, solid. Nothing can overpower such fierce possessiveness.

And God tells us we can say the same thing back. We can be possessive and say to God: "You are MINE; you are MY God!"

O

This Is MY Son!

"The angel said to her, 'The Holy Spirit will come upon you, and the power of the Most High will overshadow you; therefore the child to be born will be holy; he will be called Son of God.'" (Luke 1:35)

O

Who <u>did</u> Jesus belong to anyway?

O

Mary, a small woman, quick of step, drew her cloak close around her head and shoulders. As she hurried along, she prayed, talking to God as was her wont.

She queried God: "How did this happen? How could you let this happen to me? Did this really happen? And what has really happened anyway, God? I need some answers. I don't get this!"

Mary didn't understand a thing yet. Her mind was racing with worry and questions. She did have a certain knowing. She had a bodily knowing: She knew she carried a child in her womb—she was pregnant. The other knowing Mary had was social. She knew she was unwed—a scandal, a disgrace! She hated being in this situation and desperately wished it away, although she didn't openly let God know her secret desire to be rid of the child.

"Oh, God," she prayed. "I've always been good, faithful to the law and the covenant. How could you let this happen to me? Oh, I love Joseph so. But I'm confused, so confused. Oh God, clear my usually sane and sensible head. Please."

Thoughts of Joseph seemed to come as if in answer to her muddledness, and as she thought of their love, she began to share with God her most intimate feelings about Joseph, about his loving, warm, and powerful touch. At the remembrance of Joseph, Mary stopped walking for a moment. She looked up at the sun and folded her arms around her shoulders as if to bring Joseph's embrace into her body to help her feel safe and less alone. She stood and wrapped the remembrance of his love tightly about her as she held her face up to the Creator's sun.

Suddenly a sharp pain pierced her groin. She doubled over. "Oh God, no! No! I can't be starting to labor now. Please, I didn't mean to think it! It was only a passing thought just to get me out of this humiliating situation. I feel desperate. But I don't want to lose my baby. Oh God, save my child. Please don't let me lose this baby."

Mary sat down to rest, holding herself very still, with her hand to her belly, praying and stroking, stroking and praying, even crooning a little lullaby as if her child could hear.

Sing, my soul.
Sing to magnify the Lord,
my God who lifts the lowly
and razes oppressors.
Sing, my soul.
Sing, my soul.

Mary was doing her mothering part in the salvation of her child.

After a time, the pain subsided, and Mary resumed her journey slowly. She had to get to Elizabeth's. She needed sanctuary, a safe place to ponder and figure things out. She needed the company of another woman to talk over her tangled thoughts and feelings. But Mary kept her pace slow now and cradled her belly as she went. Her slowness made her uneasy, anxious that she might not reach Elizabeth's before nightfall. Nevertheless, she deliberately paced her steps. The baby was now more important than her timing.

"God," she prayed, "could you help me to know how this happened? I still don't understand. I mean, I did pray for this to happen, remember? I dreamed of a son. I conjured his image up in my mind, how he would look and all. I even had a vision of angels surrounding his birth. Silly! But I was supposed to be wed first! I was to be Joseph's beloved AND his wife. This is just not the right order of things at all!"

Mary's tears came as she chastised God. She was angry, confused, utterly terrified, and completely alone. And God was silent.

Dusk was swiftly descending. The stab of pain recurred, causing Mary to groan again. This time she decided to stop and rest for the night, realizing she could not go on in the dark. She found a place well off the road, hoping to hide there and be safe. She arranged a bed, a kind of a manger out of grass and brush, and lay down. She drew a piece of bread out of her pocket. As she munched on the bread, she noted its saltiness from her tears.

"Why are you so silent?" Mary asked God. "Usually I hear something, some word in my bones from you, Adonai, the Holy One of Israel, consolation of my people. Speak to me now, Holy One of blessing. Your Presence fills the universe. Your Presence fills me. Speak to me."

But God remained silent. So Mary closed her eyes and prayed for the blessing of sleep. She lay very still, hand to her belly to soothe the babe—a son, she was sure now. It seemed strange that in all of her confusion, Mary felt more and more certain about some things—like the silence of God, the life of her son, and the hardness of the ground beneath her hips.

As she lay there, she began to talk to the little one inside her. She was lonely, and he was the only one around. She talked to him in whispery, mothery lovetalk.

"You are my son, my beloved," she said. "Do you love me as much as I love you?"

She listened hard, thought she heard an answer, a little fluttery movement. She held her breath, waiting, listening intently into the darkness of her womb. Then she repeated her question, "Do you love me as much as I love you, little one?"

Something almost like a voice, but not quite, came into her consciousness. The voice said, "This is my son, my beloved in whom I am well pleased."

Mary startled, listened hard.

Again the voice came, "This is my son."

Mary didn't understand. "Who is this? What is this voice I think I hear? This is my son. Is this my son saying he is my son? These words are my words. What is this?"

Mary felt a chill run through her body. She clasped her belly tightly.

Then the voice came again, this time with stunning clarity. "This is my son, my beloved in whom I am well pleased."

"Is that you, God?" Mary asked the night. "Is this your son too? What do you mean. What do you want? This is *my* son. What is this all about? Oh God." she prayed.

Then, as if by way of answer, Mary felt a warmth begin to encircle her belly. It spread throughout her body increasing its heat. She felt inflamed, hot, burning all over. She was scared.

"Oh God, what's happening to me?"

The heat centered itself in her groin and grew in intensity. Suddenly Mary recalled her tradition's image of God as a pillar of fire by night (Exodus 13:21). She recognized the spark behind her fear as life bursting into flame. Then Mary knew what the heat was. It was the Life of God.

Then God spoke to her: "Mary, blessed are you. This is my beloved son. This is your son and your beloved, too. Will you give him to me? Will you teach him my ways? Will you teach him I am his parent? Will you love him for me? Will you forgive him his obsessiveness with me? Will you trust me to the end? And most of all, dear Mary, will you forgive me?"

Mary's resistance hit hard. Her body recoiled. She felt God calling her to give up her son, to trust and forgive.

"Give up my son? Never! Why?"

Mary argued and wrestled, wrestled and argued with the holy and burning call of God throughout the night. At times she thought it was her imagination. Or perhaps it was a punishment for some kind of sin. She even wondered if it might be an hallucination accompanying a miscarriage. Her thoughts tumbled round and round on themselves as the dark hours of the night wore on.

In the morning the light dawned softly. Mary was drenched in a profusion of sweat, but she was calm, her belly cool. Now she understood. She knew God. She patted her son gently and sat up. She took time to talk to her son. He must understand, too.

"You are my beloved son. You *do* love me as much as I love you. I know now. And you will love God, the one you will call Abba, beloved Papa, even more. I bless you, my little one. I bless you in the name of your Father, in the name of your Mother, and in the name of the Spirit of love that binds us all together. Amen."

She signed her belly with three gentle love pats and went on her way.

And so it was that Jesus was first baptized by his mother Mary in her womb.

And so it was that our sister Mary first knew the Incarnate Word made flesh in her.

O

NOTE: To read Mary's story in the Bible, see Luke, chapters 1 and 2.

Commentary

I wasn't going to write about the biblical "biggies." I had decided to stick to the "lesser" characters in Scripture and not get into the big names like MARY! But I *was*, after all, writing about women who found their spiritual authority and voice when God's Word took hold in their flesh. How could I omit Mary's birthing flesh? Hail Mary, full of grace, the Lord is with you—and so am I!

It all started in Advent, Mary's season. I was scheduled to preach, and I wanted to throw in a little of the feminine alongside John the Baptist, the traditional herald of the season. But alas . . . the parish had decided to slot in a children's Christmas Pageant on the particular Sunday I had planned to preach on Mary. There would be no sermon that Sunday.

I felt sorry for myself for a time, and then Mary helped me stretch my thinking. It had occurred to me that I could preach about Mary any old time I wanted, since Mary's season is, in a sense, eternal. But this wasn't enough for Mary. She took possession of me, urging me to find someplace to tell her story near the appointed time of the birthing. She wanted her story told! She didn't like having her appropriate seasonal time displaced. Women, she said, are displaced enough!

In answer to her call, I managed to find a church that did not have a children's pageant at Christmas, a place where I could tell Mary's story—and at the right time of the month! "What do you think I should say?" I asked Mary.

"Let's go for it!" she answered with a gleam in her eyes.

When I think of Mary, I think of the wonderful wisdom

in Toni Morrison's novel *Beloved*. A holy woman is telling her black brothers and sisters to "flesh." She recalls her people to an appreciation of fleshbound grace, a grace they can see and feel in their bodies.

> "Here," she said, "in this here place, we flesh; flesh
> that weeps, laughs; flesh that dances on bare feet
> in grass. Love it. Love it hard."

That's what Mary did. She "fleshed." She loved her flesh so hard it gave birth to God in the flesh. And the Lord God "fleshed" in Mary. What a wondrous image! Thank you, Toni Morrison. This image comes to me when I read the Isaian prophecies about rough places being made smooth and barren deserts bursting into bloom (Isaiah 40:3, 35:1). I am reminded of Mary's body and spirit bursting into flesh with God. I picture it, too, when I hear the cry of the Baptist wailing in the wilderness, "Prepare ye the way of the Lord" (Mark 1:2-3, quoting Isaiah 40:3ff). Mary comes to mind again, a woman in whose womb God digs out a holy place for God's own birthing.

Mary's person, her spirituality, and her experience places me square at the heart of the Incarnation, the Word made flesh. For me, Mary is the first incarnation. Blessed Mary, full of grace, bearing, birthing, fleshing, holy soil of God's own growth.

Of course, I often wonder what it was like for Mary. What would it have been like for you, or for me? A lot happened to that gracious lady, that "most highly favored lady," as the hymn says.

Actually, I wonder what it was like for all our biblical sisters and brothers. We are told about the events of their lives, the bare bones details of what happened to them. But we aren't told much about how they felt about their lives, how they felt about themselves or each other or their God. I suspect that the same passions moved and inspired them as move and inspire us today: love, fear, compassion, anger hope, grief, awe.

The biblical account of Mary does tell us a few things about her besides the events of her life. We know, for example, that she pondered things in her heart. We know she asked questions of angels. We know she had a profound bodily connection with her God. But we don't know how she felt, what she thought, how she prayed.

Although my story of Mary is an imaginative construction, as are all midrash stories, I believe it has its own truth. It is my understanding of Mary's passion, a glimpse at her spiritual life, a speculation about how she came to know her profound worthiness before God; how she came to know the Christ, the Word "fleshed" in her; and how her faith covenant with God, like all of ours, is grounded in mutual possessiveness.

The Spirituality of Anger

Anger is my best buddy. I love her. She has chutzpah. Her legs are short, but she has a purposive stride, too long for her small body that bounces along atop. She holds her hands on her hips to keep her torso affixed. I always know when she's coming. She doesn't come to play games much, but when she does, by God, does she know how to score points!

Which reminds me of sin. One definition of sin is "missing the mark." My best friend, anger, is always *on* the mark, so I guess she's not a sinner, as some people say she is.

God is not a sinner either. But God has a lot of wrath about being betrayed and abandoned. So do I. God's anger in me lights up my truth and fuels me to act for justice and love.

O

"Whose Life Is It, Anyway?"

And Jephthah made a vow to the Lord, "If you will give the Ammonites into my hand, then whoever comes out of the doors of my house to meet me, when I return victorious from the Ammonites, shall be the Lord's, to be offered up by me as a burnt offering."

. . . Then Jephthah came to his home at Mizpah; and there was his daughter coming out to meet him with timbrels and with dancing. She was his only child; he had no son or daughter except her. . . .

And she said to him, "My father, if you have opened your mouth to the Lord, do to me according to what has gone out of your mouth . . ."
(Judges 11:30-31, 34, 36)

○

How could Jephthah's daughter have been
so understanding about her father's sacred vow?

○

When she got to heaven, it felt like hell: insufferably tight, hot, airless!

Like the blades of a propeller, memories chopped furiously through her brain: "This is my solemn vow," he had said. "You are the object of my vow," he had said. "Alas, my daughter, you have brought me low. You, the subject of my sacrifice, the flesh of my pain, the cause of great trouble to me and the reminder of my sin."

All this he had said. All this she had believed, as if it were *her* sin. And she had felt sorry for him.

"Poor Papa," she had thought. "Always impulsive. Always so eager to please his God, to please his father and reclaim his place in the family. How many times has he told me, over and over, of his illegitimate beginnings and his triumphant return to be a warrior leader of his people, a judge. How proud and how scared he was. And how loving, too."

All her life she had heard her father bemoan his sin of fear. It was now as it always had been with him: He had opened his mouth before the Lord in haste, trying to prove his faith. He had promised a sacrifice in return for a victory. And she had been that sacrifice. A victory he had won. A daughter he had lost.

"Do to me according to what you have vowed and let it be so," she had said.

"Poor Papa," she had thought.

She knew the vow of a holy man was more important than the flesh of a lowly maiden.

But whose idea was this? What kind of vow was more important than her life?

A column of fire cut a swath through her heart as she realized the trick. Whose pain to feel sorry about? Her father's or hers? Whose wounds? Whose trouble?

"Mine," she thought. "Not his!" Tears, half-held/half-loosed, crept like lava hot down her cheeks. "It is *my* pain, *my* wound, *my* life that was quenched . . . not his, mine!"

The daughter of Jephthah stood now before the God of her people and cursed her father with unbounded passion.

She could no longer stand but fell to her knees trembling.

"Adonai, damn him. Damn my father forever for this, and avenge my soul of this injustice!"

Adonai was silent.

She lusted for revenge. It obsessed her. She had been an

innocent victim of her father's woeful and careless righteousness, his drunken piety. He hadn't even thought of the obvious: She was *always* the first one to come out to meet him and rejoice over his victories. And all this for the sake of his own winning.

"Women are always sacrificed to solve the problems of men," her sisters had told her. "This is the way of it," they had commiserated.

She thought of them now, her sisters, her friends. How they loved her. They had been with her to dance and wail and flail on the mountains. It had been a dance to life and fruitfulness. It had been the one thing she had known she had to do before she died. The women were graceful, free, alive. With their help she had experienced the fullness of her sexuality.

"Many women do not bear fruit. Many are alone. Many are empty," they had said, and they loved mightily in their lamenting. Each had embraced her, grieved her, and kissed her vigorously goodbye as she had gone to her death. She could feel even now the impress of their warm lips. The memory cooled her rage for the moment. Later, it empowered her to speak her truth to God.

Why could she not be resigned in death as she had been in life? Where was her calm resolve? What had happened to the obedient daughter, the child of the Law: "Let it be to me according to your vow?" She was Adonai's daughter now. She should be able to forgive. Why this toxic afterwrath? Adonai had avenged her father of *his* enemies. Would Adonai vindicate her now, be the Father who would be true to her, make good her name?

"Why are you silent? Can you not hear? Or are you a father just like my father? Betrayer!" she threatened shamelessly with shaking fist. "Speak!"

Adonai was silent.

Her sisters had said she would feel anger. They had also

said it would be forgiven, validated in the Presence of steadfast love and mercy. She had not believed them. She had thought she could *never* be angry at her Papa, the one she had adored, the one she had played with, the one she had felt sorry for as for a little child, as if he had been unable to take care of himself.

As a child, she had loved Jephthah's spontaneous childish ways. She had loved to listen to him talk of Adonai as he touched her face tenderly, telling her that Adonai was an even better father than himself . . . even better, she supposed, than his own disowning father. She hadn't believed it all, but she had listened to him, knowing it pleased him. She had never imagined herself as the cost of his bargaining with Adonai. A Father? GodFather?

Contempt and love warred in her breast as she saw herself, only two short months ago, running to meet Jephthah as he returned from his battles. She had felt just as she had when she was small, and he would suddenly spring up, grab her about the waist and pull her to dance and play and run with him. It was for them both an invitation to the dance of life, to enter into the careless joy of the moment.

All gone now. Gone. Dead. Finished and joyless. No more.

"He vowed me away. He paid tribute to *you*, great God, with *my* flesh. Are you satisfied with your servant Jephthah? Are you, big Lord God Adonai? Are you?"

Adonai was silent.

A sudden spirit of mockery seized her now before God, and she began to dance. She was woman now, not little girl. She danced with a heavy pounding step, determined, as if to ambush a prey. She moved deliberately, slowly at first, then faster and faster. She danced before Adonai, seductive, twisting, tossing, arching, beckoning. She abandoned herself to the Presence.

She called out to Adonai. "See me, Lord, see me dance. Am I not beautiful before you? I am a sacrifice! I am the object of my father's sin. See me and know me. I know no man, for I am a dead woman, they say."

Adonai was silent.

Jephthah's daughter at last exhausted her dance and fell. Her untamed and ravenous rage was spent, depleted.

Adonai bent down, lifted her with powerful gentleness and stood her upright. The face of Adonai shone upon her. She was held in the brilliant, enforcing gaze of God.

Adonai spoke.

"Blessed daughter. I see you. I know you. I honor you. I name you Beloved. My vow is this: Your word is now incorporated into my Word, and I will make your raging dance flesh in many women—many, many women. Beloved is your name. Never forget your name, O Woman. Remembering is resistance . . . and life."

O

NOTE: To read the story of Jephthah and his daughter in the Bible, see Judges, chapter 11.

Commentary

Like the story about the asp, the story of Jephthah's daughter was born at a writers' workshop. The assignment to write about an angry woman must have been inspirational to me because I turned out not one but two pieces on angry women. I, too, am an angry woman. I don't act angry or stay angry most of the time, but I feel angry every time I bump up against the power imbalances and abuses so prevalent in our patriarchal culture with its systems structured by classism, sexism, racism, heterosexism, and nationalism.

And why, I have wondered, do so many people condemn out of hand and/or act mystified when they encounter angry people—especially angry women? Is it so surprising that people who are depressed and oppressed feel angry? Anger threatens us because it is a fierce energy; however, anger that is spiritually grounded in the God of justice can be constructive. It is the energy that fuels creative change and keeps us from behaving as if we were helpless victims, blaming others for our plight, and refusing to see the resources God sets within and before us.

So . . . what can we do in response to ongoing, unhealed violence and innocent suffering? We can resist . . . we can be angry. It is important for Christians not to relegate the "harder" feelings, such as wrath, to the God of the Hebrew Scriptures and the "softer" feelings, such as love, to the God of the Christian Scriptures—as if there were two Gods! Throughout all Scripture, there is plenty of reason for anger at injustice, and we, with our biblical sisters, must invoke God's wrath to help us right the wrongs.

When I wrote this midrash on anger, I chose to leave
"Jephthah's daughter" unnamed as a testament to the oppression of anonymity and to the negation of being named only in
relation to a man. Jephthah's daughter said, "Let this be done to
me, according to your vow." This brings to mind a much beloved
and *named* biblical woman: Mary, the mother of Jesus. Mary was
a virgin in a different context and time. She found, as Jephthah's
daughter did, a profound connection with God in that condition.
Doctrinal history has neutered Mary and made her immaculate,
a bit out of reach. Mary, nevertheless, is beloved by many, but
most women I know love her not for her virginity, not even for
her sacred motherhood, but for her faith in the face of a painful
and difficult life. However, even posterity does not accord her
independent female status or sexuality. Like Jephthah's daughter, she is often pictured as being submissive to a "man's" plan.
Like Jephthah's daughter, the fullness of her female person is
not developed and therefore not to be known by her faithful
followers.

Mary could not change the whole system. Neither could
Jephthah's daughter. However, a very important small—and for
me, redemptive—piece of Jephthah's daughter's story is her
dying request. She was bold to ask her father for two months on
the mountain with her women companions to "bewail her virginity." Jephthah granted this stay of execution. Two months is
a long time. What all do you suppose went into this "bewailing"?
Jephthah's daughter went with her friends and seized this mountain freedom with zeal. I imagine they lamented the tragedy of
their mutual oppression. I imagine they got mighty angry. I
imagine they invoked God's wrath. I imagine they transcended
the power that oppression had over them by the simple fact of
their gathered communal solidarity.

I suspect these women rejoiced with Jephthah's daughter
in her Passion, and, all by themselves, loved her body and soul

into full womanhood, knowing, as women did then, that the loss of her virginity also meant her subjugation to a man. I suspect they empowered her spiritually to die with dignity and to carry their protest into the grave and beyond, never looking back. This is resistance at its best.

There is a very important tradition set for us by the anonymous daughter of Jephthah and her female companions, the daughters of Israel. It is written at the end of the Jephthah story that "there arose an Israelite custom that for four days every year the daughters of Israel would go out to lament the daughter of Jephthah the Gileadite" (Judges 11:39b-40).

What do we do today to uphold this call to remember our "daughters of Jephthah"? We pray. We band together aggressively rather than huddling together. We work to change cruel traditions and rewrite abusive theologies. We laugh. We rage. We share shreds of story. We coach each other. We empower each other as we support our one-step-at-a-time choices to do what feels powerful. We lament and howl at the moon. We love each other fiercely, body and soul. We claim full right to our sexuality and refuse to define ourselves simply as biological agents of reproduction. We forgive by continuing to gather and to live. And, most of all, we hold our God accountable in violently honest prayer, prayer that is energized by anger. This is the spirituality of resistance then and now.

The Spirituality of Powerlessness

Step One of Twelve Step Recovery programs states, "We admitted we were powerless over ____[insert your own item]____, that our lives had become unmanageable." This Step is the beginning of a spiritual journey toward health and wholeness.

I don't like feeling helpless. Whenever I am powerless, I feel angry. Underneath my anger dwells my fear. I feel like a tiny fish hooked on the end of a long fishing line. My powerlessness makes my life unmanageable, I decide, so I attempt to control everything and everyone in sight—and some that aren't in sight! Control is different from power. It comes from the anxious manipulations of my head. Power comes from my soul.

I have noticed, however, that every time I am powerless and I stop struggling to control, something relational happens. It may be a kiss or a prayer or a word, but something relational always happens. I am powerless but not alone.

I wonder if that's what happens with God, too? Do you think God feels powerless over human sinfulness, human shortsightedness? And then something relational happens, something like a connection for God in the prayers of the powerless. Or an intimate connection for God in the flesh of Jesus' body.

I think Jesus is God's Step One.

O

Oh, Susanna!

*Then Susanna cried out with a loud voice and said,
" O eternal God, you know what is secret . . . these
men have given false evidence against me. And now
I am to die, though I have done none of the wicked
things that they have charged against me!"*

*The Lord heard her cry. . . . she was found innocent
of a shameful deed. And from that day onward
Daniel had a great reputation among the people.*
(Susanna, vss. 42-44; 63b-64)

O

Why is <u>he</u> the hero of <u>her</u> story?

O

She ascended the steps toward heaven deliberately and slowly.
Her bones ached with length of days. She also had a bone to pick
with God. It wasn't a big bone, nor a much gnawed one, but it
was one she took from her spiritual closet to chew on occasion-
ally. She half expected to taste meat, but it yielded only carrion,
bereft of succulence or life.

Susanna felt weary as she climbed to meet God. She
hoped God would give flesh to this old bone: Why, oh eternal
God, is Daniel the hero of my story? She wanted answers. God
had heard her cry for justice in life. So had Daniel. That was
good, but it wasn't enough. She wanted *more* justice. Now God
would hear her cry again in her death. There was another wrong
to be righted. Would God give her what she wanted? She didn't

know. What she did know was that when she confronted God face-to-face, she would do it with dignity and style, for that was her way.

"Really, what I want is credit, credit for having had the courage to expose the evil doers in their scheme. I want recognition for risking my life to do it. I want it for *my* name, not Daniel's, and I want it for my sisters in faith who follow. I want them to know that it was *my* cry for justice that God vindicated, not Daniel's. I was powerless politically, but I had a voice. And a prayer! It was my cry that moved the Spirit to act in Daniel."

Susanna had been a woman of great beauty and refinement, daughter of Hilkiah, wife of Joakim. She had been a loyal daughter and a loving wife, well-trained in, and obedient to, the law of Moses. She had always felt loved and valued by her parents and by her husband. Probably it was the strength of their love that had given her the fortitude to protest the attempted rape of the elders and to choose death over defilement that day in the garden.

"But where was their courage when I stood innocent, yet accused and convicted as a liar. I was put to a shame worse than barrenness," she thought, realizing she was choking on a piece of that old bone again. "Why didn't my family speak up? That was not usual behavior for them. They weren't mutes or cowards. My God, what was this fear we all had of religious authority? Why were we all so powerless?"

She felt the old passion rise in her loins as her life review resumed. A woman of wealth and status, Susanna had carried her stature with natural grace. She had known she was the envy of many women and the desire of many men. She had not been indifferent to herself but rather had rejoiced in her body and praised God for the gift of such a fine work of art in the divine image. She and Joakim had made love with joy and playfulness, often laughing together about the silly pandering of some men, especially the elders.

The memory of their lovemaking stabbed her with sharp pain. "Why didn't Joakim come to my defense at the trial? Could it be that he actually believed their story of hiding in the garden and catching me in the embrace of another man? He knew the elders' ways as I did. He must have known the truth I told: that it was really their own lust they would have forced upon me had I not screamed out against them. Didn't he see the scheme? Or was he like all the rest, quick to cast the woman in the role of sexual sinner?"

Joakim's silence that day had been the most grievous to Susanna. Their relationship had never been quite the same. Although he had said he believed her, she had felt a haltingness in the fluidity of their lovemaking from that day forward.

"If I'd let those elders have their pleasure with me, I'd have died!" she thought. She knew that death was the punishment for unfaithfulness, but spiritual death would have been her punishment had she succumbed to the elders' cunning threat: "Lie with us, or we will testify against you that a young man was with you." Actual death would have been a preferable option.

Susanna laughed, envisioning that garden scene. She had been about to step into her bath when the two old men had pushed out through the low-lying garden shrubs that scarcely concealed their corporate bulk. They looked like two pop-up stage puppets. There they came, puffing and stumbling, leering and drooling, each trying to outmaneuver the other, while at the same time maintaining the dignified appearance befitting their office. Their judicial robes alone provided the only shred of dignity to their clumsy foray.

"I'm glad I chose life that day," Susanna thought as she looked up to see she was nearing the end of her climb to heaven. The light was getting brighter.

"It is the radiance of the face of God," she thought, "the radiance of the face of God on my face."

The closer she came, the more she felt compelled to gnaw at her bone. Her thoughts shot back again to the garden and the ensuing trial and acquittal. Even though she was grateful that her life had been spared, justice had not been done . . . yet!

"Why is Daniel the hero of my story? And will my story ever be told straight?" This was going to be her appeal to the heavenly court.

The thought of court brought sharp memories of the sham of her trial: the pretensions of the elders with their lying lips; the ghoulish fascination of the congregation eager for details; the stinging label of "adulteress" eradicating her long and good reputation with lightning-swift precision; the superfluity of the examiners, not even thinking to question the elders as to why they were in her private garden in the first place; and then her very own God-given attorney, Daniel, a mere youth, albeit handsome, bold and eloquent of tongue.

"They listened to him. They did not even hear me! My truth was ignored by my people, ignored by my family, even ignored by God."

The words of her tragic script were emblazoned on her brain:

> Hilkiah and his wife praised God for their daughter Susanna, and so did her husband Joakim and all her relatives, because she was found innocent of a shameful deed. And from that day onward Daniel had a great reputation among the people. (Susanna, vss. 63-64)

"A great reputation indeed! Daniel increased and I decreased," Susanna thought. "It's not fair! My life was radically scarred forever, and he grew famous on *my* courage—well, perhaps a little of his own too," she grudgingly allowed and continued. "I was the occasion for his rapid career ascent.

"Daniel, a sage, a prophet, wonderboy of the lion's den!

And what stings the most is that his story is recorded in the canon of Scripture, while mine is relegated like a caboose to the Apocrypha and designated as chapter thirteen. Why did God empower the man, not the woman, to be the prophet of justice forever recorded in holy writ?

"My story is a hidden writing, hidden just like my voice, my gender, my power, my advocacy for justice and due process for and by women who accuse men. Why did Daniel get the glory? Oh, Susanna, Susanna!" She clasped her hands to her head and chuckled at her own fervor. "You'll never let this one go, old girl."

At last she was at the top of the steps. It wasn't what she'd expected, but she found it much to her liking. God was in a garden, a garden rich with fruit trees, pools of clear water, gentle and colorful flowers, a garden in fact much like her own: the garden of shame and the garden of solace, her place of praise and lament, pleasure and pain, holy ground. And here was God looking more like a caretaker than an almighty judge.

"Is that you, Susanna? I've been preparing a place for you."

"It's me, God, and I have a contention, something to . . . , " she rushed headlong into her agenda, then stopped.

Susanna began an apology, then hesitated.

"Deference doesn't become you, never has. Speak on." God filled her pause.

"I have a question," Susanna said.

"Ask it," said God.

"Why is Daniel the hero of my story? And why does his story merit a whole book in the BIG book while mine is stuck off in a secondary collection, chapter thirteen no less, that isn't very prestigious or even read much? Why isn't my story important enough to be in the Bible proper?

"I thought you'd ask that. I've picked up your drift in your prayers. Susanna, I am a God of history. I bind myself this way. For my Word to be accomplished that day, I needed male flesh. I wanted to make *sure* you would live. That was the goal and your prayer too, no?"

"Well, if you're the God of history, then what about *her*story? Set it straight!"

God's laughter shook the heavens. It had a passionate quality, life-giving in depth and richness. "Oh, Susanna," God roared. "Oh, Susanna, my blessed servant, my brilliant heroine, my glory, my prophet. Oh, Susanna, daughter of my Word, how I delight in your chuzpah!"

"You have not answered my question, God. What will you do about this injustice on record?" Susanna urged.

"Well, your life was spared, was it not?" God responded.

"Not the point, but I thank you for that. This protest is not for my life; it's for the record," Susanna persisted. "I appeared voiceless and powerless, as if I had nothing to do with the positive outcome. What about all the women whose innocence was not protected and whose stories had deadly endings. Who will speak for them? They were women without power in a world where men made the rules, implemented the rules, broke the rules, and ruled about the rules! What about the women who are stained with labels like 'whore' and 'loose woman'? The women who are forgotten? They have no voice. Who will speak for them? Their cries are unheard, and now they have even been written out of history. And in YOUR book too! Besides, my own ending wasn't all that happy, you know. I was acquitted but followed from that day on by distrusting, suspicious eyes . . . even, I believe, my own husband's!"

Susanna began to weep and turned aside.

"Don't be ashamed of what you feel, Susanna, but give some credit to Daniel's discerning heart, please. He knew my desire for love and justice for all, and he spoke in that knowledge.

He is as much a prophet as you."

"But *his* name goes with that title, not mine!" Susanna responded. "What will you do about that? Will you do anything? Do you plan to set the record right?"

"I am preparing the way," said God.

"What are you so slow about?" Susanna asked. "Sometimes I think you're as powerless as women are seen to be! And I'm sick of powerlessness!"

A long silence rested between God and Susanna, as they stood together face-to-face in the garden. A very long silence.

Finally, God bid Susanna come sit down on the garden bench. God spoke softly and slowly. "Listen and hear. Even now women prophets are being born in my heart. They are birthing in my womb. Some will be writers, some speakers, some attorneys like Daniel, some counselors, some teachers and scholars, some bankers and businesswomen, some priests, some artists and poets. There is no end to the din of their voices in my creating soul. And I will speak them when the time is full. They will be heard in history. They will set the record straight."

Susanna felt a rush of youthfulness shoot through her veins. She lifted her face toward God but did not reach out or speak. She was suspicious of God's promise.

"Are you sure?" she said, aware that one last fragment of bone delayed the fullness of her joy.

God nodded. "Your story will be told in truth and in time, and you will be its heroine."

Susanna believed enough to relax; she could let go of her bone. Now she embraced God tenderly. She got up from her seat, picked a peach from a nearby tree, tossed it into the air once, and then threw it to God. They gamboled about the garden, playing catch with the peach. Susanna felt rejuvenated, reborn. Justice in its time would be done, she knew. She knew it, not just because God said it, but because she felt her own power, the power of her whole being surge within her as God looked her steadily in the eye, drinking in her full stature as if it were part of the divine form itself.

"When will this come to pass? When? When?" she asked, clapping to punctuate her words, unable to resist a last little punch at God's own good timing.

"Oh, Susanna! It is happening as we speak . . . as we speak," said God.

Then God was gone. Susanna was alone in the dimming, ineffable dusklight of the garden, her home. Content, she sat down on the grass and bit into the peach's furry skin, letting its juices run down her chin. As she rolled its sweetness in her mouth, she knew she was home, bathing in the original garden of her innocent flesh and reveling in her *own* "great reputation among the people" (Susanna, vs. 64b).

O

NOTE: To read the story of Susanna in the Bible, see Susanna in the Apocrypha.

Commentary

Susanna was a powerful woman, true and faithful. She proclaimed her pain. Yet she was disempowered both within the story itself and because of its placement in the written record: Her story is relegated to the Apocrypha (a collection of books that did not make it into the canon of Scripture that was considered to be inspired and authoritative in spiritual matters by the Anglican, Protestant, and Jewish traditions).

Professor Toni Craven of Brite Divinity School questions Susanna's apocryphal placement by the canonical editors. I wonder if they did so because of Susanna's female sexual/spiritual power? Or was it because she would not let herself be exploited sexually? Or maybe it was because, in the story, God supported her denunciation of the abuse of male sexual power. The canonical editing may have even been an attempt to keep women's voices silent.

Perhaps we should be grateful that Susanna's story at least made it to the Apocrypha. Yet even in the text of the story itself, there is an attempt to discredit her. The last lines of the book praise Susanna, because "she was found innocent of a shameful deed" (Susanna, vs. 63b). After that, there is a brief eulogizing of Daniel who gets the last word and "from that day onward had a *great* [emphasis added] reputation among the people" (Susanna, vs. 64b). That line is what stirs my juices! Why was *he* the hero of her story! Outrageous!

My mind races with thoughts, my blood with feelings akin to powerlessness. Susanna, the victim of an ingenious plot to get her to compromise herself sexually, ended up on trial for her life. How nice that they were all delighted when she was acquitted and found innocent—when she *already* was innocent! Daniel got the praise as her defense attorney, but Susanna did not get to speak at all, according to the laws of her day which made female testimony inadmissible.

Susanna, like many of us, felt utterly powerless—"completely trapped" (vs. 22), as she described it—in the face of familial, religious, and socioeconomic systems. She, like many of us, had few options. She, like us, turned to God. In God, she found power in her powerlessness. It wasn't that God found her a good attorney, it was that God's power came into her powerlessness. She found the power of her voice to cry a loud, "NO"; the power of courage to risk her life for the sake of her sexual integrity; the power of her faithfulness to declare her innocence before God and her people.

Susanna made the courageous choice to let the lies of her tormentors put her on trial for her life, rather than betray her own sexual integrity and sin against the law of God. In this, she was far from silent, crying "out with a loud voice." Her truth would be heard. As Alice Walker says in her novel *Possessing The Secret of Joy*, "If you lie to yourself about your own pain, you will be killed by those who will claim you enjoyed it."

Spiritually, powerlessness is an odd mixture of helplessness and power. God's power is made perfect in our weakness (II Corinthians 12:9). It's a paradox that is, I believe, better understood in the wisdom of twelve-step recovery programs than it is in the church. Step One is the admission of powerlessness over whatever binds and oppresses us, and every step thereafter is about God and our journey to integrate God's power into our bodies and souls.

The spiritual power in powerlessness is the power of hope. There is a difference between being helpless and being hopeless. A helpless person says, "I can't do anything about this" and turns to God. A hopeless person says, "No one can do anything about this" and turns to despair. The world may take our power away and limit us severely, leaving us helpless. But God does not leave us hopeless. When we pray, God provides hope and hope carries us through.

In Susanna's case, she was at the mercy of enemies who would have used her body for their male sexual power needs. She was at the mercy of legal and religious enemies who would have destroyed her life for their political power. She was also, ironically, at the mercy of divine power who would have her soul righteous and whole, no matter what the world did to her. It was this divine power she chose to trust.

So the powerless Susanna was powerful. She was powerful in her refusal to align with her abusers to cover their crime by demeaning her sexual purity. She was powerful in her faith. She was powerful in her refusal to be tarred with the sexual sin of adultery. She was powerful in refusing to be blackmailed by the elders' threat to testify that she had been involved in the seduction of a minor. She was powerful in risking her life and risking being raped. Susanna's power was rooted in her clear and strong sexuality, as well as her spirituality.

This kind of female power can be identified with the spirit of Eros. Eros is one of the Greek words translated "love." Eros, although most commonly associated only with romantic, sexual, or procreative love, more broadly has to do with the spirit of passion that is creative. Spiritual Eros is the creativity that happens when we connect with God and become co-creators of new things. Eros communicates through the flesh. It is sexual, sensual. It is felt in our gut, and it is what lights up our eyes as we fall in love with possibility. It is what causes us to notice new things, stretch our bodies and our imaginations. When the little flame of Eros dims, fuel for Agape is diminished. Agape is the kind of love we are more accustomed to touting in Christian circles. Agape love is the neighborly sort: charity and kindliness. But without Eros, Agape dies. Eros is the spark that we feel when our flesh jumps alive, and we connect with new possibilities for Love. For women, Eros is power and can be used to serve God, self, and neighbor.

Female sexual power is a spiritual gift. There are many other biblical women who, too, bear witness to the power of Eros in the union of sexuality and spirituality. Judith used her sexual power to save Israel and keep the tradition alive. Esther did likewise, as did Jael and Ruth and Tamar and many more. Mary, called "Virgin," made love to God Godself! We must join our biblical sisters to find God's power in our powerlessness. There is much power available for change in the collective female "NO"!

Do not lie to yourself or others about your pain. Do not apocryphize yourself. Do not give silent consent to your hidden-ness. You will be killed, in one way or another, and no one will ever know. They will think it was your will. They will think it was God's will!

Do use the power of your voice. Do raise a shout to the heavens. Do find solidarity with sisters and brothers. And do be Susanna in spirit and in truth!

The Spirituality of Begging

Most of us avert our eyes at the sight of a hungry, homeless person begging. Beggars suffer from the unattractive disease of poverty: tattered garments, tattered souls. Beggars scare me—even beggars who are little children taking advantage of their small stature to manipulate charity. I don't *ever* want to have to beg!

To beg is to ask for something for nothing, as simple charity. But isn't that what grace is all about?

On or off the street, beggary may be a spiritual gift. It takes courage to beg, to ask with energy and persistence. Serious beggary derives from profound and real need. But we are so afraid of our own and others' needs, we call even assertive asking (especially if a woman is asking) "begging," and we label it "desperate, shameful, needy, undignified, manipulative, or lazy." Labels serve to disconnect us from the truth that there are many ways to be poor.

Jesus noticed beggars. Many people in Jesus' day were embarrassed by the fact that he preferred to keep company with beggars and street people, choosing them over the more prestigious and influential, the ones who really could have financed his campaign. It would be easy to say that Jesus only liked people he could help, but I wonder. Was he trying to tell us, rich and poor, not to be ashamed of our own neediness?

God notices beggars on or off the streets.

O

Don't Settle for Any Old Crumbs!

She begged Jesus to cast the demon out of her daughter.

He said to her, "Let the children be fed first, for it is not fair to take the children's food and throw it to the dogs."

But she answered him, "Sir, even the dogs under the table eat the children's crumbs." (Mark 7:26b-28)

O

Where did the Syrophoenician woman get her nerve?

O

"Don't settle for *crumbs*! Don't, don't, *don't* settle for the crumbs!"

The thought rushed through her head like a mantra. It had been her vow at her mother's death. It was more important than ever that she not forget it now. It was a matter of life and death.

Justa was used to settling for the crumbs of life. She had been born the youngest child of many to a very tired mother. Her father had died when she was just six years old. His death had left her mother even more tired and depleted than before. No matter how much Justa did, or how attentive she was to her mother's needs, she couldn't penetrate the depressive gloom that wrapped itself around her mother. To the little child, the gloom felt alive, as if it were densely layered quilt batting that could rise up to envelop, bury, and muffle her in folds so thick she might never even see her mother again.

So Justa had kept her distance. She would stand next to her mother and wait, vigilantly, gazing from her safe stance and watching for an opportunity to snatch up the crumbs of a glance, or a word or two that might drop from the slim lemon wedge of her mother's lips. She would often ask God to make the gloom go away and warm her mother up. God didn't.

This is what Justa had done as a child. This is also what she did as an adult.

But as an adult, she felt guilty about expecting so little and settling for even less. That's why she had vowed never to settle for crumbs.

"Why are you still settling for the crumbs? It's what you always did with your mother, crazing yourself to wait on her . . . and for what? You got the crumbs of *nothing*!" That's what Justa's husband said.

And that was what she was thinking about as she sat at the bedside of her little daughter, finally at rest after a day of torment. Her husband's voice mocked her. He was right. Her slavish attentiveness had accelerated during her mother's long illness unto death. She had never stopped, trying, waiting, hoping, praying. And here she was feeling the same helplessness all over again now as she sat looking at her desperately ill daughter. She wanted to *act* in some way, do something, be different. At least the stillness of the night was giving her time to breathe, think, and relax enough to get the incessant "crumbs" incantation out of her head.

"Maybe I should seek out this Rabbi Jesus, the itinerant healer from Galilee. Maybe he could help. Would that be just grasping for crumbs again? Or a desperate denial of reality? Yes," she thought.

"No," she thought. "Oh, I don't know the difference! I

can't tell anymore if this vow is my own voice or someone else's advice. Oh God, I'm so confused! All I know is my little one needs healing now, and I hear this Jesus is from God, of God, has powers like God . . . whatever! We've tried everything. Maybe . . . if it is God . . . ? Oh God, . . . whoever you are . . . wherever you are . . . ," her voice dropped to a whisper. "I am so helpless . . . my daughter is so helpless."

Justa's thoughts trailed off. Why was she asking God for help now, when she'd always felt God dealt out only crumbs, too? She had never believed God paid much attention to her. As a child, she had prayed, but God hadn't seemed to do anything, so she had stopped praying. But she hadn't stop trying. Up to the day her mother died, she had stayed close, waiting. For what? Still waiting for the crumbs of her mother's love?

"Oh, my God," Justa thought helplessly, "here I am now, just the same: staying close, waiting. For what this time? For crumbs from God? A miracle?"

Justa didn't understand her daughter, Bernice's, illness. Its onset was sudden and terrifying. The child was thrown into fits without warning, convulsions so severe they wracked her tiny body with uncontrollable spasms before she went rigid and finally came to rest. This had been going on for two years. Justa knew her daughter was fragile. Another tumult could not be sustained. Every proposed remedy had been tried. Nothing had stayed the evil spirit of the illness. The child was in grave danger, and she was only six years old.

"The same age I was when my father died," Justa thought, remembering again the agony of her father's death, her mother's subsequent spiritual, then actual, death.

"I can't bear another death! I've got to do *something!*"

In her mind Justa reviewed her mother's dying. Maybe she could learn from it how to do things differently, how not to settle for crumbs. What she had done then was to try to prolong the ebbing of her mother's life. She had visited daily, using all her wit and energy, of which she had plenty. It was her wit, in fact, that had held her together through the losses. Her friends said her cleverness and ingenuity made her tough—and charming at the same time. She had a graceful humor, spiced with occasional sarcasm, and the gift of exquisite timing. Her husband called it her most redemptive feature.

Justa used her gift often to help Bernice get a perspective on the devastation of the seizures and to inject a spark of life into the chaos. She would devise games and little plays to help Bernice take charge of the demonizing disease. They would play "seizure." Justa would roll her eyes, gurgle from her throat, and writhe about. Then Bernice would play the role of the "Powerful Peace Healer" and come into the room with a strong, calm voice to command the demon to cease. Gradually, under Bernice's soothing touch and voice, Justa, in the role of the possessed, would calm down and slowly return to peacefulness. She would smile at her little daughter and thank her for the power of her healing presence. Bernice loved this game and requested it often. Justa didn't know if it helped, but it seemed to lengthen the times between attacks just a tiny bit, like breadcrumbs staying off an impending famine.

It was as difficult for Justa to try to stay her daughter's seizures as it had been for her to keep watch over her mother's dying. She felt just as useless as she had while waiting passively for the crumbs from her mother's life. But with Bernice, Justa felt her own efforts to be mere crumbs. She wanted to do more for Bernice than her mother had done for her. She wanted to give Bernice more than the crumbs her mother gave her.

"Did I even get crumbs from my mother?" Justa asked herself as she sat stroking her daughter's small hand, remembering how she had stroked her mother's bony hand at the end.

Suddenly her mother's dying words jumped into her

head: "Thank you, my dear daughter."

"My *crumbs*! Those were my crumbs!" Justa cried aloud. "I *did* get them. By God, I did . . . and I've overlooked their value all this time!"

Justa held her sides as the tears flowed. It was unmistakably clear. She could see her mother's face, for once the gaze unaverted, looking directly into her own face. She could hear her mother's hoarse whisper: "Thank you, my dear daughter."

"My dear daughter."

These were the crumbs of her childhood dreams, but they were not just *any* crumbs. They were her *mother's* crumbs. These crumbs were worth waiting for! Imagine ending up appreciating something you had vowed never to settle for!

It was what Justa needed. With these crumbs of affection tucked into the pocket of her soul, Justa could act. She moved with a firm step out of her daughter's room toward her own. Her vow not to settle for crumbs had been made with only half a heart. Now she knew why. Some crumbs had hidden nourishment in them. And *whose* crumbs you got made a difference. The vital remembrance of her mother's eyes, soft, supple, full to overflowing with love, took flesh in Justa and laid claim to a long-neglected daughtership. The crumbs she had passively waited for, but only now recognized for their goodness, freed Justa to act more aggressively for her own daughter.

At dawn she packed some food and prepared for the trek to find the Rabbi. She knew it was not wise for a woman to travel alone. Nor was it wise for a woman of questionable religious pedigree to seek out a prophet. But she was determined.

"However, this time I won't settle in the same way. This time I will not wait around. I can't afford the time. I will find this Jesus and see if he will give his gift to a Gentile. I will see if he is of God."

She told her husband what she intended but did not

invite him along. She wondered if he even believed she could be this nervy . . . or foolish.

As Justa walked, she took in the beauty of the countryside, the deep blue sky and the rising sun at her face. It was a day's journey from her home to the Sidon region. She found herself praying as she went.

"Oh, God," she said aloud. "Oh, God, if you are there, if you hear, if you love me, help me get my daughter well. Let this Jew be the healer they say he is. Let me not settle for any kind of rebuff, even if I have to beg. I want life, life for my beloved daughter, Bernice. I want life for her. Please God, let it be so this time. I couldn't save my mother all those years. Let me save my daughter. Oh God, I really need you now . . . even your crumbs, if that's all you can spare."

By the time Justa came to the place they told her she would find Jesus, she felt less confident. The crowds had dispersed for the night. The sun was visible only as a twilight splinter against the mountain's top. Justa felt a sudden fear as she spotted Jesus sitting alone on the rocks, gazing seaward. She approached cautiously, feeling the same yearning for connection she had as a child with her mother. She could see his face. He looked beset, tired, not as if he would have much power or time for healing.

"He looks angry. Is he angry at me?" Justa wondered. "How could he be? He doesn't even know me." She thought to turn and go home.

Familiar thoughts of self-doubt filled her head. Then she remembered her mother's voice and experienced a resurgence of courage.

"Well, he'll know me now!"

Justa launched into action, climbed the rocks, and stood at Jesus' right side, slightly behind him.

"Sir," she said softly. "Sir, I need your help."

He didn't move. Didn't he hear? She waited. She felt six years old again, paralyzed, mute, terrified.

She heard her mother's words in her head: "Thank you, my dear daughter." Then the words came out full voice: "My dear daughter. My daughter. My little girl." Justa suddenly wasn't sure if her thoughts were about Bernice or about herself.

"My little girl is ill," she said finally. "Help me. Can you heal her?"

Jesus turned very slightly, disinterested. He stared at her. She wanted to disappear at first, but then she felt irritated.

"Why is he so hostile?" she thought. "Is he going to be one of those uppity Judeans rejecting one of my kind?"

"I think you can heal her," she attempted again. "I've heard what you can do. And you look like you can. I think you can do it." Justa felt bold now, sure of herself, sure of Jesus, too, for some strange reason.

Jesus turned again to look at the sea. "No," he responded, "I've come for my people, not for yours. This is my mission. This is God's purpose for me. Be away, woman. Be away."

Justa was startled. She turned to obey. Then something clicked inside her: a chuckle. She thought what a funny little play could be made out of this now. She pictured Bernice laughing at their improvised plays. On an impulse, she turned back to Jesus, this time stepping right in front of his distant gaze.

"No," she said. "No. Look at this. Watch."

She put down her basket and removed her shawl and bandanna. Then she began to imitate one of Bernice's seizures, contorting her body and making the gurgling sounds that made Bernice ask, "Mama, is that really what I look like? It's so funny!"

Jesus stared at Justa. "What are you doing, woman? " he said angrily—but with a flicker of a smile on his lips. "Just what are you doing?"

"Look. See. This is what happens to my little daughter.

She has a demon. She looks just like this when it happens. We have tried everything. "

"But I said I have come for the lost sheep of the house of Israel first. I told you this," Jesus repeated.

Justa began again to writhe. Then she stopped. She stood straight, moved in close, leaned her body toward Jesus, her hands on her hips. She smiled, cocked her head, and said, "Ah, Rabbi, you are right—and wise, too. But let me remind you that even the dogs are allowed to gather up the crumbs under their master's table. Even the little ones who don't get the full meal are entitled and able to gather the crumbs. Even these. Even these."

Jesus looked straight at her. His gaze made her shrink, but she stood her ground under his lingering look.

Then Jesus began to laugh. He said, "Oh, woman, what wit you have! For this saying, your daughter is healed. You have loved her boldly, faithfully. You have spoken brilliantly. Go home in peace and leave me now. Your daughter is well and will grow old to one day care for you when you are old and feeble. Depart. What you have said, you have said well. What you have done, you have done well. God heals."

Justa stayed a moment longer to catch up the crumbs of his dark, kind eyes, to enjoy the connection. Then she left.

As she walked away, scarcely believing, yet believing mightily, she said to herself, "Oh, my God, I have settled for crumbs again! The crumbs from the master's table." She laughed at herself until tears flooded her eyes. "No, not the same old kind of settling . . . I *went* for them! I actually *begged* for these crumbs! Ah, but such crumbs! Not the same old kind of crumbs. Not just any crumbs. Crumbs of Life itself!"

Justa strode along in the night, feeling radiant, beautiful.

"My daughter is well. She will grow. I will teach her about life: If you decide to go for crumbs, do it boldly, in faith, and for love. And remember! There are different kinds of crumbs. Thank you, my dear God. Thank you."

She quickened her pace homeward.

O

NOTE: *To read the story of Jesus and the Syrophoenician woman in the Bible, see Matthew 15: 21-28 and Mark 7:24-30.*

Commentary

I know this woman, this little Greek, Syrophoenician woman. Oh God, how I know this woman! She represents the spirituality of beggary. She is the beggar in me.

She is the child in me who begged for crumbs of connection and praise from her parents.

She is the teenager in me who begged for attention from boys, not for her intellect but for her body, and who begged God for bigger breasts to attract that male attention.

She is the college student in me who begged the professor to understand her argument that relational values were important in ethical decision-making. "This is an essay of my own thinking isn't it?" she had said. "Yes," she was told, "but there is a *proper* way to think."

She is the young married woman in me who begged for children so she'd have someone to love her without condition.

She is also the woman in me who begged people to stop drinking, who begged God to heal her of her own abuse of alcohol.

She is the midlife woman in me who begged her church to ordain her, despite a divorce and a few ups and downs in her life.

Now she is the woman and priest and therapist in me who begs men and women in a patriarchally-conditioned church and society to listen to the little ones: women and children who fall victim to domestic violence and are trapped emotionally and economically; women and men who have been abused in childhood and whose desperate behavior is labeled "crazy," so they are drugged and institutionalized; alcoholics and addicts who strive for acceptance of their disease and all too often find rejection and shame in church and society.

Yes, I know this spirituality of beggary. I know it well. That's how I recognize it in the Syrophoenician woman, this wonderfully assertive, courageous woman who stooped to beg and whose importunity was admired even by traditional commentary on her story. She was thrice rejected by Jesus and once by his disciples. She was a noisy nuisance. She was not one of the chosen ones. She had to beg for her ethnicity to be accepted in the ruling class religious circle. She had to beg to get the healing resources of her time. She had to beg to be believed and to be heard.

She reminds me of myself—and so many other survivors of abuse and oppression. She is a survivor who begs, and not only begs but is willing to go for the crumbs in the belief that even crumbs are food and even settling for them is a worthwhile activity in God's eyes.

For many women, settling may seem to be an unattractive option, and so it is. Whenever I have had to settle for less than justice would demand, I've found it a bitter pill. However, in an unjust society, we sometimes have to settle in the short term, knowing that settling and begging are no substitute for justice. What counts in begging and settling is your motivation and the spirit in which you act. Begging must be spiritually motivated by faith (a quality Jesus acclaims in the Syrophoenician woman in Matthew 15:28: "Woman, great is your faith!") She had faith: faith in the potency of her love for her daughter; faith in the resources God gave her to act; faith in the possibility that things could be different with God's help. Settling must be done, not in a spirit of abject servility, as if it were all you could do, or as if it were all you were worth. Settling must be done in a spirit of courage, realistic humility, and yes, even cunning. And, of course, if it is done in numbers, the clamor of importunate begging does much to soften even the most squamous consciences!

The Syrophoenician woman has helped me see the spiritual value in otherwise offensive activities. Her survivorship, her courage to confront a religious authority figure and messianic contender, her humility in beggary and settlement, along with her passionate pursuit of healing for her beloved daughter, are admirable. I write about her with love. She is my hero.

I also write about her because it's always amazed me that such a scandalous little story found its way into the Christian Testament. It makes me believe that God's hand is in this for sure! Jesus doesn't come across very well here. It's embarrassing! Jesus, however, was converted by this woman's faith and by her clever argument that even the dogs, the little ones, the dregs of society, even these collect the leftover riches that fall from their owners' tables. Wasn't she clever? Don't you just love her wiles?

We could stay focused on this woman's wonderful survivorship and resourcefulness. It would make the story easier for us. We could feel inspired by this woman's example.[2] We could even sign up for the next local assertiveness training course!

We could also focus on the consoling idea that there are no leftovers in God's economy of grace.[3] As a child I loved licking my fingers to pick up crumbs. I also loved leftovers. I still do. They offer such variety to taste, and they used to make a wonderful guessing game about just what you were eating and exactly which day that week you had had that food. Fun . . . the

2   I have been made aware, particularly, of this by Chris Smith, in her tape from the Re-Imagining Conference (Minneapolis, MN, 1993).
3   See Macrina Wiederkehr's book *A Tree Full of Angels*, Harper & Row Publishers, San Francisco, 1988.

grace of leftovers and crumbs.

The holy is present in the "crumbs" of the ordinary in many different forms, often in ways that we overlook. No matter how small and momentary, these are the crumbs that give life. The spiritual eye and ear is attuned to these crumbs of grace, and thank God for that!

These foci, however, enable us to avoid facing the fact that we live in a world similar to the Syrophoenician woman's, a world of inequity, a world in which some people have crumbs while others have hundreds of loaves; a world in which patriarchal oppression and domination preside through structures of classism, sexism, racism, heterosexism, nationalism; a world in which power imbalances in domestic and societal relationships are the norm.

Yes, it is a spiritual delight to know this great, determined lady. And it is wonderful to realize that crumbs can be nourishing, that spiritually inspired settling and begging are valued in God's eyes. Yet I also ask you to look beyond all this and into the need for healing and change in our religious institutions and in our society. We really shouldn't have to have so many beggars settling for so many crumbs. I, for one, want *more* than crumbs!

The Spirituality of Envy

I've heard many a jealous spouse declare that her or his jealousy is a sign of great love. I think jealousy is really a sign of control. It's a monstrous energy that is mobilized when envy, jealousy's cousin, is lurking in the wings of one's heart, whispering the awful secret of one's own ugliness.

No wonder envy and jealousy are both identified as green: "green-eyed monster" and "green with envy." Green is the color of mold and decay. I know that when I feel envious, I am coveting someone else's "stuff." This means, spiritually, that I am living in the other's house. It's not my natural habitat. It's no surprise, then, that I decay and grow green mold on my soul. Ick!

But green is also the color of hope and new life. It is the color of the church's long green Pentecost season, the time of greening and growing in the gift of the Holy Spirit. Look carefully then at your envy to see if there are shoots and sprouts! You might find out you're not so "icky."

Don't they make healing medicines like penicillin from mold?

O

He Likes ME Best!

But Martha was distracted by her many tasks; so she came to [Jesus] and asked, "Lord, do you not care that my sister has left me to do all the work by myself? Tell her then to help me."

But the Lord answered her, "Martha, Martha, you are worried and distracted by many things: there is need of only one thing. Mary has chosen the better part, which will not be taken away from her." (Luke 10: 40-42)

O

Why is Mary's part declared "better" by Jesus?

O

" 'Mary has chosen the better part.' Oh, God, you know how I glowed when I heard Jesus say those words! I felt ten feet high, bursting with pride!" Mary thought to herself remembering that day so long ago now.

Jesus, she had thought then, had solved the problem of the sibling rivalry with one brilliant stroke. At last the "better part" had been proclaimed.

"And the 'better part' was mine. Mine, mine, mine!"

But Jesus hadn't solved anything at all. Mary's tears sprung up as she recalled the years of torment and bitterness that had continued to plague her rivalrous relationship with her sister, Martha. Jesus hadn't started the war, but he surely had done nothing to end it!

"God, how did we ever survive?" Mary continued her prayer. "It took every ounce of stamina we had. Love, too, I suppose. But praying was probably what saved us from each other and ourselves."

Mary was old now. Martha and Lazarus were dead, Jesus too, by at least twenty years. Mary had lost count as the days flowed together. She was alone now, waiting for her own death. She wasn't lonely, although her heart ached from time to time for the company of her sister, Martha. She missed Martha even more than she missed Jesus, her one-time champion.

"Champion indeed!" Mary chuckled, continuing her conversation with God. "Well, yes, for a moment he was. I needed a champion back then. I needed an advocate for my ways. I'd always felt so horribly out-of-step, guilty, and deficient. I wasn't like the other women who seemed to perform the household and hostessing deeds with ease. I needed my solitude and silence, time to think and pray and be. I tended to be annoyed by people at times, and I really *despised* domestic activity. I was a terrible cook! But, truth be told, I *was* jealous of Martha. It seemed so easy for her to do what was expected of us women. I turned my feelings of inadequacy onto her in disgust. Oh God, I was merciless in my judgment of her ways when secretly I envied them. Remember how I would pray to you to be more like Martha—more domestic, hospitable, more like a woman 'should' be? And then there came Jesus saying my ways were, in fact, the best. Oh, God, that was just what I needed!"

Mary's heart still thrilled a bit at the remembrance of that moment so long ago.

Now she found herself talking to Martha. "Oh, Martha, if you were here now, you'd say, 'Mary, stop thinking and *do* something!' You were always such a do-er. You knew how to make things feel better, to get them back in order. You were the hearth of our home. I bet if you were here now, you'd be building us a fire. Well, it's okay for me to think more now. I'm old."

Mary got up from her chair to build a fire for herself. She could build fires as well as Martha! It just wasn't what she preferred to do or instinctively did first. Likewise, Martha could think and discern, too. It just wasn't what she preferred to do or instinctively did first.

"God, remember the day Martha came up with the whole Messiah identification for Jesus? Talk about discernment! What a thing. Remember? She belted it out—no doubt about it—and in front of crowds of people: 'You are the One,' she said. My God, what a day!"

Gazing at her new little fire, Mary felt a twinge of leftover fear as she remembered how furious Martha had been at Jesus that day for not arriving in time to save Lazarus. "And right in the middle of her rage, I can still see her declaring that Jesus was the Christ. I never could have done that. All that fury, and then she calls Jesus to *do* something. Proclamations didn't matter a hair to her. She wanted action. And she got it, too!"

Bending over to blow on her struggling fire, Mary mused, "How much our relationship needed the breath of your Holy Spirit, God, to get it to fire, just to give us some light and warmth. How much. Thank You."

Mary continued her reminiscing. "I remember the long years after Jesus' death that it took before Martha and I could come to terms with our jealousies. In our long journey apart and back together again, two moments stand out in my memory. The first was the day we could bear the tension no longer. A fight was better than nothing. It began with light sniping. Angry energy fueled the fire rapidly, melting the wall that had grown up between us with its intensity. We were like two children competing for playground status. It escalated.

" 'My gifts are more spiritual,' I remember huffing.

" 'And mine are more practical, down to earth, helpful to people,' Martha had retorted.

" 'Jesus liked me the best. I'm a disciple! I listened to him so I could understand his word and explain it,' I threw back at her.

" 'Jesus liked *me* the best. I'm an apostle! I got out there and did his works,' Martha snapped at me.

"God, how awful it was. We ended in tears of frustration, each wishing we could run home to our parent of choice for comfort. But the worst part for me was the long and stunning silence of years that fell between us after that. We were afraid to fight, afraid to get close, and afraid to get too far apart. We danced a minuet of love and hate, just close enough to see each other but not close enough to touch each other."

Mary paused as she felt the weight of their separation all over again. Then she pursued the memories that haunted her: "The second memorable moment happened when I decided to break the silence. I had asked for some time to talk and Martha had consented without comment. I wanted to tell her about a new feeling I had. It was anger. And it wasn't anger at her. I was angry at you, God, for making us irreconcilably different; I was angry at our parents and the culture for setting up roles and competition; I was angry at myself—and Martha—for buying into it; and I was angry at Jesus for highlighting the polarity.

"Wasn't it just like a man, even if he is your son, to set two women up to spar over him? What is the matter with women that they can lose sight of themselves all for a word from a man?" Mary grumbled to herself and to God even now as she remembered. "Jesus might have been your son and all, but he had a lot of growing up to do!

"Getting in touch with my anger had helped me get a clear lens on things. It also helped me feel strong enough to act. I wanted to share my sharpened vision with Martha. I wanted to *do* something about this wounded relationship. So I began the conversation that day: 'Do you realize, sister,' I opened with, 'that we are silly warriors, fighting for scraps of control and validation in a man's world? Envy has been our weapon. We wanted control, but all it did was leave us enemies: impotent and disconnected.'

"I remember Martha nodding and mumbling, 'Nothing can be done.'

"I concluded my speech with, 'So, that's how I see it, Martha. I think we have been betrayed, and I think we have betrayed ourselves.'

"Oh, God, I still remember my anxiety as I awaited Martha's response. She was quiet for some time. Then she cried. Her tears flowed plenteously. I can even now see myself going over to her and feel my touching her for the first time in years. We wept. Finally, between sobs, Martha spoke to me. 'Do you know what, Mary? That's how I see it too. That's exactly how I see it. Only, for once, it doesn't make me angry, just sad. I'm glad you're the angry one this time. What a switch: you angry and powerful, me sad and vulnerable. Ha! What shall we do about it?'

"What we did about it was to spend time talking to other women and even more time talking to each other, because, even after that day, it took us time to come to peace within our differences. I still teased Martha about how she couldn't turn all this into a good deed, and Martha couldn't resist returning the snipe with, 'Nor can you analyze it accurately, sister dear!'

"Dear God, we never understood why all this had happened to us, but we did know that moment was as life-giving for us as our brother Lazarus' emergence from the tomb of death had been for him. We lived out what years we had together in peace and friendship.

"We each got a new vision, didn't we, God?" Mary prayed. "A vision straight out of the other one's 'better' parts.

You are clever."

How Mary loved to replay all this over and over in her memory. The flames of her fire were dying out now, and it was time for bed. She missed Martha, her sister and friend with whom she used to enjoy fires and reminisce.

O

NOTE: *To read the stories of Mary and Martha in the Bible, see Luke 10:38-42 and John, chapter 11.*

Commentary

A portion of a women's retreat I once led was a prayer exercise
in which I gave the women a list of about twenty Bible stories
from which to choose. Each retreatant could select and pray with
the story of a biblical sister and then create some expression of
her own identification with that character.

I was surprised to discover that a third of the women
chose the story of Martha and Mary in Luke's gospel. I was also
surprised to notice that sibling relationships were a recurring,
and energizing theme, throughout the weekend retreat. It reaf-
firmed for me that sibling relationships impact us deeply and
influence our perceptions of ourselves as faithful women.

Why so much energy around Martha and Mary? As I
asked around among other women in my life, I discovered a
similar pull. What is it in this little five-verse story that catches
our attention? The Martha/Mary story clearly has power. Too
much power? Perhaps it troubles us, makes us wonder about our
ways of faithfulness: Would Jesus approve of the way we live?
Which is the "good" part and which is not? Perhaps it activates
old, and perhaps denied, feelings about siblings, especially sisters. For centuries, the story has set up shame, confusion, and
power struggles, both internal and external.

I began to be troubled myself. Did Jesus *really* say that
one way was better than the other? That doesn't sound like
something he'd believe. It must have been Luke's agenda, I
concluded. To feel supported in the direction of my thinking,
however, I checked out the text[4] and found that this story was
not a red-letter (i.e., "Jesus really said this") text. In fact, it wasn't

even marked pink (a "probably authentic Jesus-saying"); or even grey ("Jesus didn't say this, but the ideas are close to his own").

I believe Luke wrote these words as Jesus' words to make a point. The conventional wisdom of the day was that women were relegated to serve in the kitchen—as Martha did—but not to listen to Rabbis, study and learn, pray and proclaim the gospel teachings—as Mary did. And by having Jesus affirm Mary, Luke could portray him as affirming the ministry of all women disciples. Regardless of who said what, it was certainly characteristic of Jesus to punch through the conventional wisdom of the day to offer a new perspective, a different and liberating way of seeing things.

Still, it troubles me. Even if Mary's part was validated, look where Luke ascribed the power! It was with the woman who did what the men did, and, further, it was with the woman who sat at the feet of a man who had more power.

And look at what happened relationally. It was not, I think, characteristic of Jesus to be unkind or to set up rivalry, especially among his faithful followers. Jesus loved the family in Bethany. I don't think he would have humiliated Martha in front of everyone. This would have been, in fact, a painful manipulation for both women. Mary might have gotten to bask in her glory for a moment, but perhaps she later fell back into her accustomed guilt and uncertainty about herself for not meeting the prescribed role expectations of her day.

Of our day, too? I know many a "Mary" who feels unfaithful because she doesn't spend much time in the kitchen, doesn't serve on the Altar Guild, or isn't a social activist.

---

4   I refer to the translation of the Jesus Seminar group, *The Five Gospels: The Search for the Authentic Words of Jesus*, new translation and commentary by Robert W. Funk, Roy W. Hoover, and The Jesus Seminar, Macmillan, 1993)

For Martha, who was only doing what was expected and what she probably liked (except for not having enough help at it), the proclamation of who was "better" would have also been a set-up for insecurity and self-doubt. She got criticized for her performance anxiety, for wanting everything to be "just right" for the meal. I'd want the same thing, if Jesus were coming to my house for dinner! I'd be anxious, too! Wouldn't you? But I know many a contemporary "Martha" who struggles with the belief that she would be more faithful if only she were able to be more like the thinking "Mary."

Jesus might well have confronted either woman about her compulsivity, as he did with Martha, but in the spirit of compassion, I think he would have done it privately and not in the context of comparison. And he would have been sensitive to the sibling dimension of their relationship. (Incidentally, if you think Mary does not have a compulsive side, let me enlighten you. We more easily understand Martha's busyness and compulsive activity in the context of American culture. But Mary can be compulsive, too: when she sits and studies and learns, and takes just one more workshop, reads just one more book, or takes just one more course before she speaks or acts. That's compulsive Maryism!)

So . . . although I understand Luke's agenda and the point he made, I fervently wish he hadn't made it a Jesus quote! Oh, how I wish he hadn't had Jesus say it in just this cruel little way. Oh, how I wish the women weren't typecast so stiffly. They were pawns in a man's story. They were symbols, passive recipients to Jesus' "thumbs-up/thumbs-down" evaluation.

And, oh how I grieve that it is still this way today for so many women. Too often we live in envy and behave jealously. We await the approval of our culture, of our church, of our men. We fail to trust our own gifts. We betray each other, acting out, over and over, rivalries such as the one set up in the story. We compete for the blessing, jockey for power and position, see each other as enemy. We dislike or fear each other. What a waste of our energy, especially at a time when we need solidarity to use our considerable gifts to work for peace and justice; to maintain the gains already made in the economics and politics of equality; and to emphasize relational wholeness and mutuality, not difference and competition.

I do, however, take some consolation in other words Luke attributed to Jesus: Mary's part will "not be taken away from her" (Luke 10:42b). I presume, therefore, that Martha's part would not be taken away from her either. Both parts are spiritual. Both are valid. Both are valued. Both are necessary for the spread of the way of Jesus and the living of the Great Commandment.

The Spirituality of Death

The Bible is right: Death stings![5]

When my daughter was a small child, she developed a very big—too big—fear of death. It preoccupied her. It was taking away her life. I felt inadequate. I didn't know how to help, how to give her faith. I didn't know how to give her God! But, of course, I couldn't give her God. All I could do was listen, hold her and love her. Eventually, that was enough . . . maybe it even was God.

What is so scary about death? Why do our young defy it and the rest of us deny it? We talk about death in the church, but not *really*. Crucifixes, if they are present at all, are often stylized. We forget that the Eucharist began in the slaughter-house. We turn our funerals into Easter celebrations. Let's face it: We're afraid. If we let death sink into our bones, it does sting, because we know that to die is to cease to exist as we are; to die is not to know what comes next—except by promise. Fear is entirely appropriate and normal.

There's a scene in Terry Tempest Williams' book *Refuge* in which the daughter lies next to the mother and breathes her, breath by breath, out of life and into death. She did a beautiful thing. I learned years ago, from my daughter, that only when love—no matter how meager—intermingles with death can our fear of death be quieted. I guess that's why the Bible talks about death and love so much in the same breath.

O

5   Hosea 13:14 LXX; I Corinthians 15:54-55

Is Love Enough?

She has done a beautiful thing to me. . . . She has done what she could: she has anointed my body beforehand for burying. And truly I say to you, wherever the gospel is preached in the whole world, what she has done will be told in memory of her. (Mark 14:6b, 8-9, RSV)

O

What is this good news we tell "in memory of her"?

O

The pain was less—now that she had her plan. The plan had come from much thinking It had grown slowly, creeping like grabber vines across the thickets of her brain. Now it was settled in her gut, enwombed, ready for birthing. It was hers. It was a delicious plan, bold and passionate, born of a love stronger than death.

She thought about her plan as she worked on her pot. Her fingers curled lazily around and around the soft clay, etching gentle crevices into its suppleness. She thought about her plan and its formation. She smiled wisely and with pleasure untinged by complacency.

She had always been a thinker. Thinking had seemed a good thing to her, as good as creating with her hands, maybe even better. Thinking was an inner thing. Outer things people could touch or break or destroy with their tongues. But unuttered thought was safe. No one could take it away or mutilate it.

For her, it was like a prayer. Only God knew her inner strivings
and connivings, and God was safe . . . most of the time.

It was not safe anywhere else for women to have thoughts
or strong opinions. Even as a child, she had been hushed. Her
curiosity had been seen as an offense, her questions, assaults;
therefore, her ideas found no birthing place. They had been as
useless as her pots—"just" for beauty and pleasure, no more, no
less. Her way of thinking and creating was *not* the way of the
Lord, people had told her. The way of the Lord for women was
to serve at table, or at cradle, or both. Neither suited her. She
was different, maybe even strange.

"The strangest thing about me is that I've never thought
I was strange," she thought and frowned.

She had listened and listened to this one called Jesus. His
thinking was like hers, except that his thoughts came out of his
mouth, and hers stayed in the secret chambers of her heart. She
remembered how she hadn't trusted him at first. He was a man,
after all, the ruling kind, the kind for whom women were silenced
and constrained to serve.

But Jesus taught that women could follow by serving *and*
by thinking—even by creating pots instead of scrubbing them.

He wasn't a traditional man. "Different, like me," she
thought.

Yet Jesus did do servant-like things.

"What that *really* means is 'woman-like' things!" she
thought with disgust, then caught herself being contemptuous
of women.

Her rapid-fire hostility stung as she recalled one particular woman-like thing Jesus had done for her: He had washed her
feet. It had happened when Jesus and his band of gypsy-like
followers had returned to Bethany after a long day's trek. That
day she had been in the group. It would have been usual for the
women to wash the men's feet and then their own, but Jesus had

done things differently. She looked down now at her feet where the memory of his touch still lived. It had been at that moment of washing that she had fallen in love with Jesus. It was then that her plan had been conceived, fueled by love, constructed by thinking, and now soon to bear fruit.

She hadn't risked this kind of love for years, but now she would put her plan into action. Her plan, she thought, would finally answer her lifelong question: Is love stronger than death?

The question had come out of a death. Thirty years ago she had loved. She had loved her sister with a love that was deep, secure, unshadowed. She remembered her joy when her sister had come into her lonely, young life. As a child, she had had nowhere else for her heart to go. The older ones seemed preoccupied. They didn't want her thoughts, or her love, so she had lavished it all on her sister. But after four short years, her sister had died.

The loss had left her broken, had kept her from loving. She vowed never to risk love again. Love hurt too much. It was why she'd never married, never had a child. She had never invited the marriage of love and death . . . death had always won, leaving love impotent in its wake. The more alive and hotter the love, she had learned, the deader and colder the death.

Even now as the memory surfaced, her loss cut through her brain like a scythe through dry wheat. As she worked her pot, it flowed through the ends of her fingertips, becoming one with the clay and with the conviction she held of things yet unseen. Her decision to enact her plan would settle the love/death question: Which was stronger?

As a child, she had been taught that God's love was stronger than death, and that this love lived on in God's faithful people through the generations. Her experience told her this was not true. She had loved God with all her heart and her sister as God's own. But the power of that love had not been stronger than death. It had not lived on at all. It had died just like her sister. Love died. She had painfully learned that death was stronger than love.

Her hands pressed with increasing vigor into the yielding clay. The pot was taking on a life of its own, a new life that blended with the shaping movements of her hands. Hands and clay formed one life.

"How much I loved that little one. She was my life," she found herself saying to the emergent pot. "How much. How much. Was it too much, do you think?" she queried wistfully. "God, how many times have I asked you that? I thought love could save. I thought my love for the little one, the one I mothered for my mother, the one I fathered for my dead father and in your name . . . I thought my love could overcome death. If love were stronger than death, it could stop death, couldn't it? I was so sure, so sure."

She knew these to be childish wish-beliefs. Her sister's death had taught her that love was pretty powerless. Yet she still held tenaciously to a vision that there might be a love stronger than death. "If only my love had been stronger. If *my* love could have saved her, she wouldn't have died!"

Now, however, there was something about Jesus that had reawakened her dead love, changed her mind. It was something none of the others liked about him, but she did: She liked the way he talked about love and death in the same breath. For him, the two went together, just as they did for her. But Jesus did not seem stifled by the association, as she had been. He was not spiritually defeated and lovelost as she had been for thirty years, and he never ceased making the love-death connection. It was compelling to listen to him, eerie, in fact. Whenever she and the others spoke of loving Jesus a lot, he spoke of death; and whenever they spoke of death and fear, he spoke of love, new life. The others did not seem to appreciate the connection, but she did.

It re-enflamed her curiosity and her ability to love. The memory of Jesus' enlivening touch, still lingering in her feet, made the promised connection feel so real. Slowly, slowly, as the pot was forming in her hands' now-gentle caress, she began to see Jesus' point, to understand the paradoxical connection.

"I have a second chance," she thought. Carefully she cleaned up her hands and placed a damp cloth over the as-yet unfinished pot and began to ready herself for the short journey to Bethany. "I didn't believe in my sister's death, only in her life and what it gave me! This will be a different love, a love not so selfish, a love that allows for death. And I will do this love with my hands. As with my pots, I will create new life out of dead clay with the love in my hands. With my hands I will anoint his body before his death. He will take into death my love pressed into his very bones and flesh."

As she walked through the dusky glow of approaching night toward Simon's home in Bethany, where she knew they would be gathered, all these thoughts seemed to enter into her hands as they slid back and forth against her hips. Drawing closer now she could hear their laughter and talk coming from the house.

"They know only love, not death," she whispered as she stood in the doorway listening, looking, smiling, seeing Jesus listening, looking, smiling. "He knows life. But he also knows death. So do I."

Then she entered the room. She moved forward toward Jesus. He saw her coming and smiled at her. She carried her anointing perfume in a small jar at her side. It hung on a leather thong and bumped gently against her thigh as she strode toward him.. The others fell away, stunned, then grumbling; hushed, then agitated. She reached Jesus, stood before him. Her fingers sought the contents of the jar at her side, and her hands began the work of anointing.

As if Jesus were a clay pot, he yielded to her hands' working life into his skin with love. His skin was warmed as she rubbed her perfumed ointment into it. Her hands moved along the lines of his face, tracing the care-lines, massaging the hollows of his cheeks, smoothing the darkening veins of his neck. She worked downward over his arms and shoulders. She could feel him relax, easing to her fingers' strokes. His breath came heavy on her face; his eyes closed to shut out the increasing clamor.

She anointed with passion, not noticing the others. It was as if she were working the death out of his very skin with her act of love. She almost began to believe that *this* love could be stronger than death.

She finished. Sweat formed on her upper lip, but her countenance was smooth, questionless, stunning. Jesus nodded, thanked her, even as his eyes groped for more of her touch, not wanting to let her go. But she was finished. She turned to go.

The others now were shouting for her life. She had done a wasteful thing, they said—scandalous! But she heard nothing. They closed in with curses upon the woman whose perfumed love was an anointing for death. Her way was obstructed as she tried to move through the crowd to leave.

Jesus saw the danger and spoke, silencing them with his anger. "Leave her. Leave her. She has done what she could, a beautiful thing, anointed me for death with her love. Do as she does in remembrance of her."

His words gave her enough time to edge out of the house. She didn't look back or hesitate but went on out into the night: anonymous woman, weeping in death, laughing in love, rubbing her hands firmly now over her own body in remembrance of the One whose love she knew *was* stronger than death.

O

NOTE: *To read the story of this Anointing Woman in the Bible, see Mark 14:3-9.*

Commentary

Falling in love with Jesus the man started for me with the Anointing Woman portrayed in Mark's gospel. Mark's version[6] is especially important to me because of its anonymity and also because of the particular relational portrait this writer presents. The Marcan image fits with my spiritual need for a mutual relationship with Jesus and others in my life.

I spent a year or more praying contemplatively with this story. Spiritual healing took place in me as I prayed with this courageous and loving woman, letting her shape my identity and experience as I prayed. I experienced healing for my tendency to become dependent on others to give me my sense of myself by doing too much or being too nice at the cost of my own needs. Jesus' statement, "She has done what she could," contains a liberating definition of ministry: Do what you can, where you are, with what you have to give. No more and no less. It's that simple and that pure. It's properly balanced according to self, God, and neighbor. And it's not codependent!

---

6   Note: The story of the Anointing Woman is reported similarly in Matthew's gospel, chapter 26. However, Luke's account (Luke 7:36-50) and John's account (John 12:1-11) are quite different. In Luke's account the woman is more servile, portrayed as a penitent sinner, weeping and washing Jesus' feet with her tears. This image is an alternative view appropriate for some people at certain times. The woman in John's gospel also crouches to anoint Jesus' feet and is identified as Mary, the sister of Martha and Lazarus. This identification ties the story into the raising of Lazarus tradition and clouds the relationship issues. Both Luke and John omit Jesus' astounding proclamation of this woman's ministry as gospel itself! It is also of note that the Lucan and Johannine texts are principal service selections in the Episcopal Book of Common Prayer lectionary, whereas the Marcan and Matthean versions are excluded as principal service readings.

I also experienced spiritual healing in my relationship to men. In this story I could not "spiritualize" Jesus. He was a flesh-and-blood man. I was forced to confront his maleness. I was forced to confront my own femaleness. I had been dead to my own body. With the help of the Anointing Woman, I was able to love my body out of death, just as she had done for Jesus. I was able to feel my sexuality and to feel it affirmed without shame or exploitation. Because Jesus was so open about his intimate connection with God and with this woman, I felt my person, both in deed and flesh, to be wholly acceptable in God's sight and before men.

What is remarkable about Mark's account is Jesus' affirmation of the woman's action: "Truly, I tell you, wherever the good news is proclaimed in the whole world, what she has done will be told in remembrance of her" (Mark 14:9).

With these words, Jesus consecrated the woman's act of ministry. Just as the sharing of bread and wine in the Christian Holy Eucharist is to be done in remembrance of Jesus, acts of "anointing" (loving touch) are to be done in remembrance of her. When we remember in direct, physical ways, we re-embody the love that death seems to have taken away. We are to do as this woman did so that her remarkable blend of love and death will be as spiritually present among us as Jesus' love-death connection is in the remembrance of the Eucharist.

I guess this must be why I wore my father's tattered and outsized old golf sweater around for a time after he died! It gave me a bodily remembrance that made his love more present than just a memory.

The Anointing Woman is present for me every time I consecrate bread and wine. I remember her. She is also present for me every time I touch someone in Christ's name, when I make a deep and healing connection with the Spirit of God in another.

I remember her as the one who discovered divine love's potency in her body and in Jesus', through her anointing action. I remember her as the one whose silent, healing touch bore the truth of a love stronger than death, a love that took the dreadful fear out of biological annihilation.

What is equally remarkable to me in Mark's story is the relational mutuality portrayed between Jesus and this woman. I like the fact that she *stood* before him as he sat at table, a posture of confidence and connection. Her body stance empowers me in my relationship with God and with people. It assures me that I am "worthy to stand" before God.[7]

The Anointing Woman has helped me to know with certainty what it means to be a "christ." These days it is difficult to know what a Christian is. Frankly, it is difficult for me to advertise that label, although it is branded into my soul by Baptism and by adult confirmation. I was recently at a church diocesan convention where I overheard some people say, as they pored over the slate of candidates, "Which ones of these are the Christians?" They wanted to make sure they voted for the "Christians" at an official all-Christian event. I remember momentarily wishing I weren't a Christian, whatever that is!

But I remembered the Anointing Woman. She was not a Christian, by whatever understanding. But she was a "christ," a mediator of truth and love. I learned from her that one does not have to be a Christian to be a "christ." In her and in Jesus I have come to know God's affirmation, and I am unafraid to stand before men with my power, my gifts of ministry, my truth, and my womanness.

Thrilling also to me is this woman's prescience, her early recognition of Easter in the man before her. Jesus welcomed her

7   This phrase is part of one of the prayers of consecration, Eucharistic Prayer B, The Holy Eucharist Rite II of the Episcopal Book of Common Prayer.

ministrations. He acknowledged her because she did not deny the reality of his death but chose, instead, to anoint his death with her love. While the others were busy planning more ministries for the poor and the next chapter of the Jerusalem coup, this woman was emotionally honest enough to declare her compassionate and passionate love for Jesus. She was also honest enough to anoint his body beforehand for death, knowing that the fate of crucified bodies was vultures and dogs. Her gesture was courageous, bold, and filled with hope. I see her anointing as a sign pointing in hope to the resurrection of Jesus' body, an act that only divine power could accomplish, an act that this woman foreshadowed. She believed in it through Jesus before he died and lived again. For me, she is an example of true Christian faith, the faith that believes in the historical Jesus as the manifestation of God.

She is also an example to me of christian ministry. Her action bore the marks of true christlove: to do what we can with what we have where we are; not to be in denial of reality; and to have the courage to act on our heart's discernment of what true holiness is in the moment. Authentic "christs" are often shunned as inappropriate rule-breakers. They can be unpopular. They may not always be nice, helpful, dutiful people. They, as the Anointing Woman, are often the scandals of their community. But they are true ministers of the Christ, as Jesus so aptly noted.

True ministers, or authentic "christs," take risks for the love of God and in God's name. There is always death lurking and skulking around the edges of this kind of love, not only for those who are dying and in need of love but for the givers of love as well. Love-givers like the Anointing Woman must relinquish cherished and long-held rules and ideas about themselves and their roles, behaviors, and boundaries. They risk death by destruction or death by ostracism.

Many think it is a great grace, as well as a bewilderment,

that Jesus gave the anonymous woman in Mark's gospel such approbation. John Dominic Crossan in his book *Jesus, A Revolutionary Biography* wonders why Jesus gave her "such a stunning accolade." Crossan speculates about the authorship of the gospel and suggests that this woman could be the "Mark" who wrote the gospel, signing herself obliquely and indirectly into this story through Jesus' affirmation of her act.

"We cannot ever be sure," Crossan writes, "whether Mark was a woman or a man. We can, however, be absolutely sure that the author of this gospel chose an unnamed woman for the supreme model of Christian faith—for the faith that was there before, despite, or even because of Jesus' death."

But is all this really so appalling, astounding, and "stunning"? A woman as "the supreme model of Christian faith"? A scandal of grace, to be sure, but not a surprise. The Anointing Woman, like Jesus, knew about the love-death connection. She profoundly understood the spirituality of death. We know she knew it by the way she acted. For her, as for Jesus, love *is* there before, despite, and because of death. You might even say her love *did* find a way to overcome death!

Suggestions for Personal Prayer and Meditation/Group Rituals

For each chapter, personal prayer and meditation guidelines, as well as suggested group rituals, are offered to expand your use of this book and your understanding of the Scriptures.

The prayer and meditation suggestions are guides for your personal prayer time. It will be helpful to have a journal or notebook at hand. Be free in your prayer and open to what happens.

The group ritual suggestions may be used by any group of people who are reading this book together and meeting to share. It will facilitate the group process if the group members have spent individual time with the prayer and meditation suggestions before gathering. The directions are written for a group facilitator, who may be one designated person or a rotating leader from the group each week. Remember that, in any group exercise, people always have the option to participate simply by listening and presence without sharing.

Chapter One:
The Spirituality of Laughter

The Story of Sarah in Genesis

Suggestion for Personal Prayer and Meditation

▶ Read the Abraham and Sarah story in Genesis 18:1-15, slowly, aloud. Notice your feelings as you read.

▶ Write your thoughts and feelings in a journal or notebook.

▶ Recall a time in your life when you or others felt your laughter was inappropriate. Envision that time in your imagination as you bring it before God in prayer. What memories come up for you about the role of laughter in your life?

▶ Record any insights you receive in your journal.

▶ Think for a moment about what you are praying for now in your life? What big stresses and problems are you facing? How do you need God to be present with you at this time? Ask God for the strength of laughter in your faith and see what happens.

Suggestion for Group Ritual

Here are two rituals, one on age and one on laughter. Use both rituals or whichever ritual seems to fit the experience of your group at this point.

RITUAL 1

▶ Ask each group member to write her/his age on a slip of paper. Ask each one to think whether age has ever served them as an excuse to refrain from saying or doing something they knew was important to them.

▶ Direct each person to add a brief description of the graces of their particular age. For example, "At ___ [age] ___ , I am _____ , and I can_____.

▶ Collect the folded slips of paper in a basket. Pass the basket around, asking each member to draw a slip and read it aloud.

▶ After everyone has read, spend five minutes in silent prayer. Then ask each member to say a brief prayer aloud for the person whose slip they read. For example, "*God, I pray for the person who is 56 . . .*"

RITUAL 2

▶ Ask each member of the group to tell a joke or to share a funny incident or word from their life experience. Help the group enjoy the laughter by encouraging them not to worry about being "pious." Suggest to the group that they think about God and Jesus laughing. You might even pose the question, "*Don't you think God and Jesus laughed together sometimes?*"

Chapter Two:
The Spirituality of Shame

The Story of the Snake in Genesis

Suggestion for Personal Prayer and Meditation

▶ Read the story of the snake in Genesis 2:4b-Genesis 3, slowly, aloud. Notice your feelings.

▶ Recall an incident from your childhood when you felt like the snake in the midrash, as if everything in the world were your fault. Envision yourself as that child. Let that child be present before you. Be aware of your feelings toward that child. What kind of relationship do you have with that child now?

▶ Write your thoughts and feelings in your journal or notebook.

▶ Is there a relationship in your life now in which you feel stuck? Does it have to do with shame or blame? Pray about that relationship, envisioning that person in your mind's eye as you bring him/her into your space with God.

▶ Write a prayer, or a psalm about your prayer experience, in your journal.

Suggestion for Group Ritual

▶ Place a candle along side a flat rock in the midst of the group. Explain the meaning of the symbols to the group as you arrange the objects: The candle is a symbol for the Spirit; the rock represents the old lady asp's rock.

▶ Ask the members to sit in silence and contemplate these symbols for about ten minutes.

▶ Then ask each member of the group to share one thought or feeling from their contemplation. It might be something that moved them, or pained them; it might be awareness of a place where they need grace in their lives; it might be an insight derived from personal prayer and meditation time. (Remember to remind the group that when sharing is asked, there is always an option to pass.)

▶ Close the group time by having each group member say: "*I place on this rock my need for*_____." After everyone has verbally placed a need on the rock, have each person extend a hand toward the rock. Lead the group in saying this blessing prayer together: "*Loving God, in your mercy, bless our needs.*" This can be repeated several times until it fades naturally.

Chapter Three:
The Spirituality of Possessiveness

The Story of Mary, Mother of Jesus, in Luke

Suggestion for Personal Prayer and Meditation

▶ Read the story of Mary in Luke 1:26-56, slowly, aloud.

▶ Notice what you identify with in this story. Notice in particular any one word or phrase in the story that pulls at your heart, causes you to feel a jolt of energy. It may be a place of spiritual connection for the Word of God being announced in you.

▶ Write down the word or phrase that catches your attention.

▶ Pray by repeating that word or phrase over and over again, both silently and aloud.

▶ Record your thoughts and feelings about the word or phrase in your journal or notebook.

▶ What might God be announcing to you through this word or phrase? Journal your reflections.

▶ Write your own Magnificat, offering a prayer of praise to God.

Suggestion for Group Ritual

This ritual needs a bit of advance preparation. Ask members ahead of time to prepare for the group meeting by thinking of a child in their life, a child from whom they have felt disconnected or lost in some way, either by death or estrangement. The child may be one they need to let go of, or one they never had, or it can be any child—even themselves as a child. Ask everyone to bring to the group meeting a photo or an object that symbolizes this child.

▶ To begin the ritual, give the group a few minutes in silence, asking members to envision their child in their mind's eye.

▶ Ask each member briefly to share something about their child, describing him or her to the group, showing the photo or object they brought, and explaining how the child has been lost.

▶ After each person finishes speaking, direct them to place their photo or object into the center of the group.

▶ Ask each member to baptize and bless their child, making the sign of the cross, or other meaningful sign, on the child and on themselves, in this way:

> "_____, my child, I name you, I bless you, and I possess you, in the name of the Holy One whose presence fills the universe, whose presence fills me. And I baptize you in the name of God, Creator, Christ and Holy Spirit. You are mine and you are Christ's own forever. AMEN."

(You may wish to use another prayer or blessing, according to group needs. This is only a suggested wording. It is always an option for anyone to participate simply by being present without sharing.)

Chapter Four:
The Spirituality of Anger

The Story of Jephthah's Daughter in Judges

Suggestion for Personal Prayer and Meditation

▶ Read the story of Jephthah and his daughter in Judges 11, slowly, aloud. Notice your feelings.

▶ What memories does this story evoke in you? Have you ever felt like a "sacrificial lamb"? Do you think God came to your aid in any way? Where do you need God's aid now?

▶ Do you think God listens to you when you're angry? How might God be a part of your anger?

▶ Write about your thoughts and feelings in your journal or notebook.

Suggestion for Group Ritual

▶ If possible, build a small fire in a fireproof dish and place it in the middle of a table around which the group sits.[8] Dim the lights.

▶ Ask the group to gaze into the flames for a brief time, imagining that the flames are the wrath of God turning heat onto the wounds of the world to cauterize and sanctify them.

▶ Then ask each member where their own wounds are. Suggest that they go inside and identify the wounds in their bodies and then imagine the divine flame of wrath touching them in their place of woundedness. Encourage each to feel the heat, to feel God's burning, healing touch in their bodies.

▶ Ask each group member to share an occasion in which being wounded evoked anger in themselves, and/or in which they wished for God's participating wrath at whoever or whatever wounded them. After each sharing, maintain a period of two or three minutes of silence.

▶ At the end of that silence, if it is safe to do so, direct the sharer to place a small piece of paper into the fire with the words, *"God, I am angry at _____ ."*

▶ Then ask the sharer to lead the group in reciting together this prayer:

> *"God of all wrathfulness, bless this woman's anger.*
> *Let it burn to purity in this flame."*

---

8   An alternate suggestion is to create a fiery sense by placing several candles close together.

Chapter Five:
The Spirituality of Powerlessness

The Story of Susanna in the Apocrypha

Suggestion for Personal Prayer and Meditation

▶ Read the story of Susanna in the Apocrypha, slowly and meditatively. Take particular note of your emotions as you read.

▶ After you have read the story through once, return to the places in the story that aroused the most emotion in you. Breathe deeply into your body. Notice the presence and flow of your energy. Where do you feel tense or relaxed? Take an inventory of your body from your head to your toes and notice where energy is blocked and where it flows easily.

▶ As you sit quietly and let your body speak to you, allow whatever emotion that wants to rise to the surface.

▶ Recall a time or times in your life when you felt powerlessness. How did you experience powerlessness in your body? What emotions for you are connected with powerlessness? What did you do about your situation? Did you pray? Write your feelings in your journal or notebook. Let yourself experiment with "body praying." Begin by moving your body into whatever position feels most safe and comfortable to you. You may even want to place your hands on the parts of your body that feel powerlessness, pained, or tense and pray the Spirit of healing into those parts. If you feel able to do so, try praying naked. How do you experience the Spirit moving in your body? As you are praying in this way, be aware of God's presence with you in your body, asking God to bless your body and your feelings.

Suggestion for Group Ritual

▶ Ask the group to share some experience, either from their personal prayer and meditation time or from another occasion, in which they have felt bodily powerlessness. Ask them to consider if they feel that God loves them in their bodies. In their sexuality? When they are powerless?

▶ At the end of the sharing, ask everyone to stand up and stretch. Have everyone focus on something they wish to say "NO" to.

▶ Then ask everyone to take four deep inhales and exhales. After the fourth inhale, have everyone shout, "NO!" on the final exhale.

▶ Repeat the same process with a focus on something people wish to say "YES" to. Take four deep inhales and exhales, and on the last exhale, have everyone shout, "YES!"

▶ Close the group with a litany. Ask the members to stand in a circle and participate in saying the following litany about herself/himself, with the whole group echoing back after each individual statement:

Individual:	*I am a woman (or man)!*
Group:	*You are a woman (or man)!*
Individual:	*I am powerful!*
Group:	*You are powerful!*
Individual:	*I am* [say own name].
Group:	*You are* [say individual's name]!

▶ The litany is complete after everyone has had a turn to make their individual statements and be echoed.

▶ End the ritual with a group shout of "AMEN!"

Chapter Six:
The Spirituality of Begging

The Story of the Syrophoenician Woman in Mark

Suggestion for Personal Prayer and Meditation

▶ Read the story of the Syrophoenician woman in Mark 7:24-30, slowly and aloud. (You can also find the story in Matthew 15:21-28, if you want to read another version.) Notice your thoughts and feelings.

▶ Say a brief prayer asking God's Holy Spirit to lead you into understanding as you pray with this story.

▶ Read through the following imagery suggestion:

> Envision the scene of the biblical story. Notice the colors, sounds, smells, sights. Take in the whole scene. Breathe it in deeply. Place yourself into the scene wherever you fit or identify. You may be an observer, a disciple, the woman, or Jesus himself. Let yourself become the person with whom you identify and let the scene unfold before your eyes, playing it out in your imagination and including any dialogue that emerges.

▶ Now sit in silence for a few minutes, breathing and inducing a state of deep but mindful relaxation. Close your eyes and begin to let this imaginary scene take shape in your mind's eye. Let it play itself out as long as it will.

▶ After you have opened your eyes and returned to the present time and place, write down some of your thoughts and feelings in your journal or notebook. What do think is God's Word for you in this story?

▶ What crumbs do you desire from God? Pray for them.

Suggestion for Group Ritual

▶ Plan ahead with your group for a Eucharist or Agape service. Ask members to bake some homemade bread for the feast. If you plan a traditional Eucharist and there is no priest among you, invite a priest to celebrate with you who will allow you to do all the planning and give you the flexibility you desire. Otherwise, plan together an informal Agape meal in which bread is broken and shared, along with prayers, readings, and music as you wish.

▶ Use the Syrophoenician woman's story in Matthew as the reading. Ask someone to read the story aloud. After a brief silence, ask the group members to share their thoughts and feeling about the story.

▶ Focus the group's attention especially on the breaking of the bread. Ask them to notice what happens to the crumbs that fall. Encourage them to feel the crumbs of the eucharistic bread as they consume it, to feel its texture on their tongues and in their mouths. You may want to say these words: *"Take time to taste, chew, swallow, and feel the holy bread go into your body to nourish you."*

▶ After the eucharistic ritual is finished, let the group decide what is to be done with the remaining crumbs or pieces of bread.

Chapter Seven:
The Spirituality of Envy

The Story of Mary and Martha in Luke

Suggestion for Personal Prayer and Meditation

▶ Read the story of Martha and Mary in Luke 10: 38-42, slowly and meditatively. If you know the story well, it will be tempting to skim it. Reading it aloud might help you to hear it with more freshness.

▶ Notice what attracts or repels you in the story. Write down some of your thoughts and feelings in your notebook or journal.

▶ If you have a sibling, focus on him or her and let yourself consider your feelings toward your sibling. (If you have more than one sibling, you may do this for each of them or pick the one who first comes into your thoughts.) Remember how it was for you in your childhood, if you have lived together as children. Notice how it is for you today.

▶ If you do not have a sibling, think of someone who is most like a brother or sister to you and focus on the history and nature of your relationship. Also notice what feelings you have about not having any blood siblings.

▶ Imagine you and your sibling, or chosen sibling, standing with Jesus. What needs might you each make known to Jesus? What sins might you each confess? What healing would you each desire from Jesus? Notice how it feels to "listen" to your sibling, or chosen sibling, speak intimately with Jesus. How does it feel to have him or her "listen" as you speak to Jesus?

▶ Place your sibling, or chosen sibling, before your mind's eye and pray with her or him, asking God to fulfill your sibling's heart's desire.

Suggestion for Group Ritual

▶ Ask the group members to share either from their prayer and meditation experience or from some personal reflections on the relational issues of the midrash. Ask people not to comment after each sharing. Each sharing is a gift offered freely and with trust into the safety of the silence.

▶ This can be a very emotional and life-giving experience. It also may be anxiety-provoking, especially if there are siblings, or chosen siblings, present in the group, or if anyone in the group knows your sibling, or chosen sibling. Remind group members that there is always the option to share just by listening, praying and being present.

▶ After each sharing, maintain a minute of silence. Ask each member during the silence to pray in silence with the person who has just shared.

▶ If you have access to Edwina Gateley's book *Psalms of a Laywoman*,[9] it might be an enhancement to read "The Sharing" after your sharing.

▶ Close your group time with the passing of the Peace, directing members to say to each other:

> *"The peace of God be with you, sister* [or brother].
> *And with you, sister* [or brother]."

9   Gateley, Edwina, *Psalms of a Laywoman.* Source Books: Trabuco Canyon, CA, 1988, p. 65

Chapter Eight:
The Spirituality of Death

The Story of the Anointing Woman in Mark

Suggestion for Personal Prayer and Meditation

▶ Read the story of the Anointing Woman in Mark 14:3-9, slowly and meditatively.

▶ Take particular notice of your bodily sensations. What does this encounter between the woman and Jesus arouse in you? What remembrances do you have in your life of love in the face of death?

▶ Write down some of your thoughts and feelings in your journal or notebook.

▶ Where and how do you see God's presence most clearly in this story?

Suggestion for Group Ritual

You may do one or both of the suggested rituals. One is specific to the midrash. The other is a closing ritual for the time your group has spent together reflecting on this book.

RITUAL 1

▶ Prepare your group ahead for this exercise of *descansos*. Talk a bit about the meaning of *descansos:*

> "Descansos *in Spanish means 'resting place.' You can see* descansos *if you travel in the southwest. They are symbols, often little crosses, that mark places along the road where a death has occurred. It is important to mark the deaths or losses in our lives to give recognition and peace to our sorrow and to celebrate the ways in which we have experienced resurrection and new life. A death may be biological, accidental or not, or it may be a time in our lives when we have felt halted or been forced to change our direction."*

▶ Ask the group to prepare at home by drawing a time line of their lives and marking each loss with a cross. Suggest that they make the crosses large or small, colorful or plain, according to the emotional significance of the loss. If a loss feels resolved, tell them to write "forgiven"[10] over the cross marker. If it is not resolved, let it stand on its own. Ask the group to bring their time lines to the group prepared to share one or two *descansos*. For each *descanso* to be shared, ask each member to bring a cross (it can be made out of paper or any other material) to represent the *descanso*.

---

10   "Forgiveness" here means canceled, no longer binding, as a debt. When a loss is forgiven, the pains surrounding its impact no longer have any emotional and spiritual hold on the person. No more payment is required, no more time and energy needs to be deposited in the grief bank and kept away from the living of one's life. One's soul is detached from the loss and re-attached to oneself.

▶ At the group meeting, gather the group around a table. Ask each member to place the cross that accompanies each *descanso* onto the table and to share something about it.

▶ To close, ask all members to extend their hands over the assembled crosses and say together:

> *"Bless, O God, these crosses, symbols to mark our descansos. For those that are not forgiven, bring peace. For those that are forgiven, receive our thanks. Amen."*

RITUAL 2

▶ Before the closing meeting, ask group members to bring a symbol of what the experience of reading and sharing the midrashim in this book has been like for them. It could be a midrash of their own, a piece of music, an icon, or a piece of artwork, something from nature or an original creation.

▶ Spend your final group time sharing the symbols.

▶ You might decide as a group to end this session using a litany. The group as a whole can decide the content of the litany. (See the litany on page 119 for one possibility.)